"The best book on networking I've read in a LONG time! Rob shows you how to win in every aspect of life by teaching you how to be a master at the networking game... and does it in a book that can be read in one sitting. Read it... use it. Win!"

Todd Falcone, *Network Marketing Speaker, Coach and Author*

"*The Game of Networking* is the modern day book for *How to Win Friends and Influence People*. It dives deep into specific skills that are all too often just skimmed over. And most of all, this book is REAL LIFE. After building a network of over 150,000 distributors in 5 countries, I can tell you that Rob knows the game of networking. His examples are real and his stories are compelling. Great book!"

Jordan Adler, *Author of the Amazon Best Seller,* Beach Money, *Network Marketing Millionaire*

"Unique, well written, simple to read, everyone on the journey to a better life will find nuggets to better their effectiveness in the world!!"

Dan McCormick, *35 year industry leader, multi-million dollar earner and co-author of* Lessons from Great Lives

"Rob Sperry's *The Game of Networking* is a wonderful tool to add to your business toolset. His formula makes the necessary, but often times difficult task of networking obtainable. Sperry's principles are easy to understand and this book will certainly give you the skills to improve your networking ability in all aspects of life, not just business."

Ty Bennett, *Author of* The Power of Storytelling

"It is rare that I get an opportunity to read a fresh new powerful material on the subject of networking. This book is rich with stories, research and powerful distinctions. Studying it (vs reading it) will result in a quantum leap on your leadership, reputation and success. When it comes in print I will be gifting one to all of my teammates.

Congratulations Rob. This is a fantastic work of art."

Richard Bliss Brooke, *Bestselling Author of the Network Marketing book* The Four Year Career®

D0829629

"*The Game of Networking* is not a good book... it's a GREAT book! It's one of those "buy first" books that literally stands out among it's peers. I love the constant references to history, to current influencers and the wisdom they all bring to this great profession.

But it's the mindset training that makes this book stand out. It goes beyond the necessary skill training to that never talked about area of why we need to learn it to do it. The actual science behind it all. And with his real time references, the reader can see the results of doing what it takes!

I have been doing this for a very long time and I learned a ton. What was exciting for me was knowing my new people and my biggest leaders are going to get great benefit from the same book!

My advice. Buy it. NOW."

Tom Chenault, *Host of*
The Tom Chenault Radio Show *and million dollar*
annual earner in Network Marketing

"The ONLY book you ever need to read about MLM and building a real business fast and solid. No fluff- the real stuff. Simple and straightforward. Rob is the REAL DEAL."

Lon A. Wardrop, *30 year Network Marketing*
veteran, multi-million dollar earner and legendary recruiter

"Rob's book is filled with insight and strategies that can be used in any industry. Rob lays out a thoughtful formula for increasing likeability, which in turn equates to higher credibility. I've been able to follow his strategy to successfully increase my own networking reach and influence within my industry."

Trent Lee, *Multimillionaire, Serial Entrepreneur*

"Entertaining and easy to digest. The intent behind this book is genuine and oozes off every page: to share what works, what's fun, what duplicates, and what's profitable so you can shorten your growth curve in the exciting profession of network marketing."

Josephine Gross, *Editorial Director,* Networking Times

"Finally a book that drops the hype and gets right to the essentials of network marketing! Rob Sperry is a master at breaking down the things that matter most in simple ways that you can apply and benefit immediately. Must read for any professional at any stage of their career!"

Brandon Carter, *Owner, Solar Company*

"These time-tested techniques need to be in every Networkers pocket if they wish to uplevel their business. I only wish I had had a copy a decade ago!"

Rachel Jackson, *Internet network marketer. Has made $3.5 million in 6 years in the network marketing industry. Rachel is a masterful online builder who bridges the gap between "high tech" and "high touch."*

"Having worked with Rob on a daily basis for most of a decade, I can attest to Rob's metamorphosis into one of the great networkers of our time.

His ability to not only transform himself into a great networker is amazing, but his ability to break down the steps into a duplicable game so that others can do the same is truly remarkable.

This book will teach you how to create, maintain and grow meaningful connections. Rob will teach you how to provide value for others so they want to be in your network. He will teach you the skills and disciplines to begin your own metamorphosis today!!

If you are going to only read one book on networking, this is that book. It will help you not only become successful in your MLM business, it will help you become successful in all aspects of life."

Lance Conrad, *Entrepreneur, Network Marketing multi-millionaire, Consultant*

"Every once in a decade a new book comes out that changes an industry. *The Game of Networking* is that book for this decade. Rob as pulled together the steps to go from where you are to where you want to be."

Woody Woodward, *Author, Success Strategist, Film-maker*

"Put simply, Rob Sperry loves people and has a passion for service to them. That love and passion fills every page of his new book, *The Game of Networking*. Rob dives deep into what it takes and exactly how to become a great networker. He shares real life experiences mixed with proven stories to illustrate the significance of (relationships/friendships). This a powerful, must-read book."

Lisa Grossman, *Network Marketing Speaker, Consultant and Strategist*

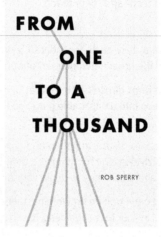

FROM ONE TO A THOUSAND

ROB SPERRY

Download my free eBook on how
to never run out of contacts

www.robsperry.com/blueprint

THE GAME OF NETWORKING

BY ROB SPERRY

TGON Publishing

TGON Publishing

Warning—Disclaimer

The purpose of this book is to educate and inspire. This book is not intended to give advice or make promises or guarantees that anyone following the ideas, tips, suggestions, techniques or strategies will have the same results as the people listed throughout the stories contained herein. The author, publisher and distributor(s) shall have neither liability nor responsibility to anyone with respect to any loss or damage caused, or alleged to be caused, directly or indirectly by the information contained in this book.

ISBN #978-1-64007-484-2

WHAT IS IN IT FOR YOU:

During my years of research I have asked some of the top leaders in the industry for the formula for networking and I have read hundreds of books on the matter. I have come up with the 3½ Laws that will enhance your networking skills to increase sales, revolutionize your relationships and build a referral engine.

The top inventors, visionaries and mavericks all used networking to launch and leverage their companies. Whether it was Thomas Edison networking with Henry Ford to put his batteries in Ford's cars, or it was Steve Jobs networking with George Lucas to acquire Pixar or social change like Bill Gates and Warren Buffet networking and creating the Giving Pledge, which has generated more financial contribution than any other charity in history, these visionaries used the 3½ Laws that I illustrate in this book.

You will benefit in the same way they did, to create lasting change, exponential growth and massive success.

CONTENTS

INTRODUCTION

I want you to take a few minutes right now to think about everything of value in your life. Think of your family, your relationships, your home, your car, your education, and your overall net worth. Believe it or not, all or most of anything you consider valuable came from networking. Everybody networks. However, not everyone networks well. Networking doesn't have to be something that you are simply born great at or not. Networking can be learned. Networking is a science. Networking is a differentiator for success.

This book will teach you all that life can offer you as a professional networker, including: learning how to get out of speeding tickets, how to maximize social media, how the Law of Credibility will help you get to the top ranks of your profession in half the time, how the Benjamin Franklin effect will help turn foes into friends with one question, the importance of building your brand, where and how to meet people, how to become the host of events (even if you are an introvert), how to network like a superstar without being that annoying schmoozer, how to make a great first impression with a few simple tips, how to effectively communicate with anyone in any situation, and much, much more.

Additionally, you will learn networking skills from legends such as Johnny Appleseed, Bruce Wayne, James Bond, Katniss Everdeen, Luke Skywalker, Darth Vader and Jay Gatsby. I will use real-life examples from my own personal experiences as well as experiences from many of the world's top network marketers who have collectively earned well over hundreds of millions of dollars. Simply put, you will learn the best from the best. Not only will you learn from this book but I have a Facebook group called The Game of Networking. In this group you will not only learn from me but from many other top industry leaders. This is where you can stay plugged in on the latest content.

Jimmy Fallon once sat crying in the back corner of a Carl's Jr. restaurant. He had been rejected for yet another acting gig, and his future looked bleak. Even though Jimmy is currently the widely viewed, super successful, and downright hilarious host of "The Tonight Show," he struggled massively at the beginning of his career.

In this particular situation, although Jimmy was struggling he was not out. He continued to submit audition tapes to different agencies, hoping for something to stick so he could finally launch his acting career. He had submitted an audition tape to Saturday Night Live, and he got the call back saying that he had been accepted to be in the cast. While on SNL, Jimmy made sure to thank its creator, Lorne Michaels, after every single show. This built a strong relationship that helped Fallon when he left SNL to pursue a movie career many years later. Even years after SNL, Fallon made it a point to stay in contact with Lorne Michaels.

After a few unsuccessful years in the movie business, Fallon felt stuck and reached back out to his mentor, Lorne Michaels, for some advice. When Michaels was looking for a replacement for Conan O' Brien's place in his "Late Night" TV show, he offered Fallon the position immediately because of their relationship. Years later, when Jay Leno was retiring from "The Tonight Show," which aired an hour before "Late Night," Fallon was promoted and took over the spot, and the rest is history.

Jimmy Fallon's story is a perfect example of how well-maintained relationships can help someone pursue their happiness and leverage their talent. He developed relationships and grew a network that ended up contributing to him reaching the pinnacle of his career. Even though Jimmy was turned down again and again, he made sure to be a likeable person with a good attitude; he built his Credibility by never giving up and continuing to work in the broadcast and media industry. He made sure to increase his Recallability by staying in the minds of those people important to him, and all of these things together led him to eventual success and profitability. Jimmy purposefully set himself up in positions to network so he could advance his career. He used what I call the "3½ Laws of Networking" to do so, which you too will learn about by reading this book.

This book isn't about how to invite, follow up, or close. It's about putting the networking back into network marketing. You will learn very specific, proven strategies throughout the book, and many of these strategies will be brand new to you.

How can you NOT be that crazy annoying type of network marketer?

How can you recruit the masses?

How can you have unlimited contacts?

How can you turn enemies into friends?

How can you connect with successful leaders?

How can you brand yourself?

How can you partner with other network marketers and learn from them?

How can you build a true residual income and achieve your goals?

How can you expand network marketing into an incredibly larger network?

You may not realize it now, but everyone loves networking. Yes, even you. To me, networking is creating, developing, and maintaining relationships to create opportunities to enhance your life and the lives of others. Throughout the networking process, you will gain a set of skills that can be applied to any situation and improve your chances of having a multitude of success.

So, go ahead and ask yourself this question: Why are you networking? It seems like a simple question, but this is one of the most important questions you can ask yourself. If you set out to network primarily to find new prospects for your network marketing business, then you are going to learn a lot from this book. There is so much more to your networking than just a potential person for your downline, and this book will give you that better and broader vision; guaranteed.

I have been writing this book on and off for over seven years. I don't know if you should be embarrassed for me or impressed by me. Can you imagine writing a book for seven years? I have read hundreds of books to better understand the theories behind many of the concepts in this book. The more I wrote this book, the better I understood what networking is all about. I began to think about networking in depth and ask myself these questions:

How did I meet my wife?

Networking

How did I get involved with network marketing?

Networking

How did I find where I wanted to build my house?

Networking

How did I build a large tennis program?

Networking

How did I find a great deal on my car?

Networking

How did I find an orthodontist for my kids?

Networking

I could go and on and on and on, but you get the point. Networking can be considered the most important skill but very few of us are ever taught specifically how to do it. Have you been taught specific advanced strategies on how to network? If networking is widely known as being one of the most important skills for success, why is it that we are rarely taught advanced strategies on how to improve and cultivate these skills?

I still haven't met anyone who can give me a great, three-minute explanation on how to effectively network. By the end of this book you will have learned the 3½ laws to be able to properly explain the formula for networking in 3 minutes or less. Each time I read a book or article on how to network, it gives some great ideas, but every single time it is missing a few important aspects to the full strategy of networking. I was begging for a simple strategy that sums up how to network successfully. I searched unsuccessfully and I couldn't find one. So, I've spent the last 7 years learning and reading all I can, then applying what I learned. This book represents those real world lessons.

It all boils down to 3½ laws of networking: (1) Likeability, (2) Credibility, (3) Recallability, and (3.5) Profitability. The laws are simple, but the execution is difficult.

I count Profitability as half a law because many people assume a deal is done when they've learned the first three factors. Sure, networking is first and foremost about relationships. Networking isn't about the 'short term' gain that any specific relationship offers. It's about the Game of Networking. However, if you aren't optimizing your network effectively, in financially beneficial ways (that are win-win), you're missing out.

I promise you that you will learn principles about how to network in a way that you have never heard before. These 3½ laws will give you an in-depth take on exactly how to network, and by the end of this book you will think differently than you do right now. Your personal growth, just from reading this book, will be tremendous.

Learning how to network is so important that I believe this is the first book anyone in the network marketing industry should read. The principles taught in this book will help you in so many ways beyond just your network marketing business. This book will be a blueprint to help you succeed in whatever drives you.

CHAPTER 1

THE LAW OF
LIKEABILITY

LAW #1

James Bond is known as a British spy who can escape any difficult situation while still (somehow) expanding his coolness factor. He manages to win at everything he does. He is a world-class gambler and seems to play for the mere pleasure of winning, not really caring about the money. He always wears the sharpest suits and tuxedos. He is physically fit, and he has that likeable smile, a unique charm, and contagious charisma. He knows how to get what he wants, and even some of the women that play hard-to-get fall under Bond's trance.

Although he isn't perfect by any means, Bond uses many of the Rules of Likeability to get what he wants! Likeability isn't everything, but it is the first step in becoming great at networking.

THE IMPORTANCE OF LIKEABILITY

The following paragraphs draw from the book *The Likeability Factor* and give a fascinating take on being likeable:

It may seem that the Likeability Factor is something you are just naturally born with, but it is actually a skill set that you can develop. Do you think it's a worthy skillset to develop? Well, here's what I know about likeable people.

- They are more successful in business and in life.
- They get elected, promoted, and rewarded more often than those who are less likeable.
- They close more sales and make more money.
- They get better service from people like doctors and health care providers.

1

A Columbia University study by Melinda Tamkins shows that success in the workplace is guaranteed not by what or whom you know, but by your popularity (creating popularity usually means creating a network). In her study, Tamkins found that popular workers were seen as trustworthy, motivated, serious, decisive, and hardworking and were recommended for fast-track promotion and generous pay increases. Their less-liked colleagues were perceived as arrogant, conniving, and manipulative. Pay raises and promotions were ruled out for those less-liked regardless of their academic background or professional qualifications.

Can you believe that? It doesn't matter whether someone is better qualified by formal education. Once you are in the same setting as another individual, your ability to move up and get pay increases depends on your Likeability Factor, NOT your academic background or qualifications.

Gallup has conducted a personality factor poll on candidates in every presidential election since 1960. It measures three things: issues, party affiliation, and Likeability. In the 2016 presidential election both candidates hit historic levels of unlikeability. Although likeability has been the #1 determining factor on final election results, this election was different. The majority of the public didn't like either candidate and the majority voted against the one they disliked the most or for whom they felt would make a real change.

Need some more proof? Doctors give more time to patients they like compared to patients they don't like. This was proven in a 1984 University of California study. The significant differences in treatment, according to the doctors themselves, depended on the combination of being 'likeable and competent.' Those patients who were just likeable or just competent were not encouraged to call in for follow up appointments as often as those patients who were both.

Mark Jackson was the coach of The Golden State Warriors from 2011 to 2014. He inherited a terrible team his first year and turned that team into a playoff contender in his following two years. When he was fired in 2014, most were shocked. Joe Lacob, the Golden State Warriors owner, said this of Mark Jackson: "Part of it was that he couldn't get along with anybody else in the organization. And look, he did a great job, and I'll always compliment him in many respects, but you can't have 200 people in the organization not liking you." Mark Jackson wasn't fired for his coaching. He was fired for being unlikeable.

Mark Jackson isn't the only big-name person that has been deemed "unlikeable." In 2012, four years after the greatest US economy meltdown since the Great Depression, the economy was supposedly the #1 most pressing issue for Americans voting in the next presidential election. Polls fluctuated but every poll showed Mitt Romney with a substantial lead over Barack Obama in polling numbers for who would be a stronger president for helping the economy. Obama may not have had the publics' trust on the economy but he absolutely dominated Romney in the polls for being more likeable.

We all know the end result. Despite what was claimed to be the #1 most important issue, growing the economy, it still couldn't supersede the Likeability factor. In a post-election analysis, many experts pointed to Likeability and empathy as the major reasons for Obama's victory. In an article analyzing election results, ABC news said the following: "Obama trounced Romney by a 10-point margin in being seen as 'in touch' with average Americans. But for the one attribute that Obama won - the candidate who 'cares about people like me' — he beat Romney not by 9 or 13 or 23 points, but by a whopping 63 points."

I think we can all agree that becoming a likeable person is well worth it. How do we take that to the next level and actually execute our skill set to be more likeable? The following rules will guide you to be more likeable.

FIRST IMPRESSIONS LAST FOREVER, SO DON'T SCREW IT UP

To be successful, you have to be able to relate to people; they have to be satisfied with your personality to be able to do business with you and to build a relationship with mutual trust. — George Ross

The first time I met Curtis Broome he had just emceed the "Go Pro Recruiting Mastery" event for the previous three days. Since he was the emcee of the biggest network marketing event of the year, naturally everyone wanted to shake his hand and rub shoulders with him. It was midnight and Curtis had lost his voice. I knew Curtis had to get up early the next morning, and I knew he was beyond exhausted.

As I was introduced to Curtis, I was greeted with a huge smile, a solid handshake, and some humor. Curtis then spent an hour with me and a very small group just shooting the breeze. He was very personal, sharing stories about his life and showing genuine interest by asking me numerous questions. I walked away late that night in awe of the strong first impression Curtis had made. He was fun, confident and yet very personal. No matter how tired you are, remember first impressions can last a lifetime. I know mine of Curtis will. I have kept up my friendship with Curtis, and in large part I attribute that to the lasting first impression Curtis made on me.

First impressions are created within the first seven to thirty seconds of meeting someone. Once you understand how critical first impressions are, it is vital to realize the importance of your smile. Your smile can have an immediate impact on how someone judges you for the first time. I once read a quote that said this about the value of a smile:

It costs nothing, but creates much good. It enriches those who receive it without impoverishing those who give it away. It happens in a flash but the memory of it can last forever. No one is so rich that he can get along without it. No one is too poor to feel rich when receiving it. It creates happiness in the home, fosters goodwill in business, and is the countersign of friends. It is rest to the weary, daylight to the discouraged, sunshine to the sad, and nature's best antidote for trouble. Yet it cannot be bought, begged, borrowed, or stolen for it is something of no earthly good to anybody until it is given away willingly. —(Author Unknown)

Make an extra effort to show genuine interest in someone else immediately. Make an extra effort to not only smile but to also mention their name immediately. Your job is to always make others feel important and the easiest way to do that is to call someone by their name. You should make a conscious effort to go above and beyond in making others feel important the first time you meet them. Make a lasting impression on the first impression.

HOW I GOT OUT OF NINE SPEEDING TICKETS

First off, you are probably wondering how I managed to get myself pulled over nine times for speeding. That's a story for another day! To focus on how I put the Likeability rules into practice, I will go into detail about one traffic stop in particular. Now, this method of getting out of speeding tickets is not fool-proof!

I start off by thinking how I can be more likeable in the officer's eyes. I always have my license and registration ready in hand. I immediately show a remorseful facial expression. I make sure my tone is sincerely sorry, and I do mean it. I always take responsibility and say that is definitely my fault. Police officers are used to most people taking no responsibility. They are used to people arguing and yelling at them, so take the opposite extreme. Officers are used to unpleasant, unaccountable, and unlikeable people. Nine out of the last ten tickets I got out of were because I did the exact opposite of what police officers usually deal with. I am likeable even when getting a ticket, and most of the time it makes all the difference.

The one ticket I did not get out of still bothers me to this day. I'm not bothered because I didn't deserve it; instead, I'm bothered because I didn't even have a chance to apply my techniques! This particular police officer pulled me over, walked right up to the car and told me I was speeding. He then proceeded to take my license without ever making any direct eye contact and without engaging in any conversation. My powers were gone!

I had no chance, and my wife was laughing at me saying, "It was about time!" Then, the officer walked back to my car and handed me my ticket. As I drove off, I thought either this guy is socially clueless or he is brilliant by not engaging in any conversation. Either way, I got caught, and the police's actions (or lack thereof) were my kryptonite!

While this story may be humorous, it is important to note how I made a conscious effort to be likeable. At the end of this law, I will teach you the specifics of becoming more likeable. I am not kidding when I say that I have gotten out of nine speeding tickets by doing exactly what I described above! It is so easy to overlook how far you can go by avoiding confrontation and just be likeable. The only time I wasn't able to use my powers, I got the speeding ticket!

Conversation is a major key to being likeable. Knowing how to communicate, which is much more than what you say, will make a big difference. You can't simply look good and have a smile on to be likable. You must also know your audience. You must treat others as they would want to be treated.

LEADER OF ONE, LEADER OF MANY

*No matter how busy you are, you must take time to make
the other person feel important.* —Mary Kay Ash

One of the greatest books of all-time is *How to Win Friends and Influence People*. My biggest takeaway from it was the difference between humans and everything else is our need to feel important. This is such a simple, yet profound, insight that gets to the very core of becoming likeable. If you want to become likeable and truly make a strong connection with others, then make them feel important. That's it!

The way to do that is to figure out what makes an individual tick. What makes them feel important? Another interesting read that will help you better understand people, communicate better, and make others feel more important is the book *The 5 Love Languages*. *The 5 Love Languages* goes into depth on how to treat others based on how they want to be loved. Contrary to popular belief, this isn't just for dating or marriage. This book will help you better understand yourself and others. It will help you communicate better with others because we all communicate differently. Most of us treat others based on how we would like to be treated rather than how they would like to be treated. In other words, it teaches you how to make others feel important.

In fact, let me tell you the story of a friend of mine, Derek Tillotson, who has mastered exactly this. He doesn't do so in a loud manner, nor does he do so in a way where he throws out constant compliments. He does so in a way where he is always positive about everything and everyone. He never puts other people or companies down and makes others feel comfortable being themselves. Derek has been around the network marketing industry his entire life, and he still manages to be the best at what he does.

It doesn't matter if Derek was born with some innate quality of making others feel important, or if it was taught to him, or if it is both. Derek has a way of making everyone around him feel important. If you met Derek, you wouldn't know how successful he is. I say this with the utmost respect. He is unassuming and talks very little about himself always focusing on making others feel important.

Likeability is one of the most underrated skills. While we tend to judge ourselves by our intentions, others judge us by our actions. It is their observations and conclusions that shape their perceptions. Others' perception is their reality. Don't underestimate the value of being likeable.

THE BEN FRANKLIN EFFECT

One of the easiest ways to make others, especially enemies, feel important is to implement the little known technique called "The Ben Franklin Effect." Very few, extraordinarily special individuals have heard of this psychological phenomenon (say that three times fast!). Franklin said that those who do favors for us like us more. He even goes on to explain that by asking even your enemies to do a favor for you, it helps them to like you more. The phrase "I need your help," goes a loooooooong way.

In his autobiography, Franklin explains how he dealt with the animosity of a rival legislator when he served in the Pennsylvania legislature in the 18th century:

Having heard that he had in his library a certain very scarce and curious
book, I wrote a note to him, expressing my desire of perusing that book, and
requesting he would do me the favour of lending it to me for a few days.
He sent it immediately, and I return'd it in about a week with another note,

expressing strongly my sense of the favour. When we next met in the House, he spoke to me (which he had never done before), and with great civility; and he ever after manifested a readiness to serve me on all occasions, so that we became great friends, and our friendship continued to his death.

It is simple: ask someone for a favor and they will like you more. People like helping other people. People like being needed as long as you don't take advantage of them by asking for too many favors. When someone does you a favor, there is a magic to it. There are a couple of principles to understand why the Ben Franklin Effect works.

First off, we love what we serve. The more you serve something, the more you tend to love it. Of course I love my parents a ton, but I never realized how much they loved me until I had kids. Changing diapers and dealing with kids throwing up and whining isn't fun, and anyone that tells you it's not a big deal obviously doesn't have kids. Kids are rough at times, as they need so much attention from their parents, but they also bring their parents so much happiness. As you serve your children you grow attached to them. Sacrifice is the ultimate sign of love. The more I serve my kids, the more I love them. We love what we serve.

Next is the fact that even if someone doesn't like you, when they end up doing a favor for you, they find a way to justify why they like you. They do this because they feel the need to justify why they are doing you a favor.

Last, but not least, when you ask someone to do a favor for you it is a compliment. You typically wouldn't ask someone you hate to do a favor, so asking someone to do you a favor is a sign of respect. You are letting that person know that you like and respect them. Just remember to not take advantage of others by asking for too many favors. If you abuse the Ben Franklin Effect, you will lose its ability to strengthen relationships.

Jeff Bezos, the founder & CEO of Amazon.com, gives insight into how he created a "loved" company in his memo entitled, "Amazon.love":

Rudeness is not cool.	*guys is cool.*
Defeating tiny guys is not cool.	*Inventing is cool.*
Closed following is not cool.	*Explorers are cool.*
Young is cool.	*Conquers are not cool.*
Risk taking is cool.	*Obsessing over competitors is not cool*
Winning is cool.	
Polite is cool.	*Empowering others is cool*
Defeating bigger, unsympathetic	*Capturing all the value only for the company is not cool.*

Leadership is cool.	*Authenticity is cool.*
Conviction is cool.	*Thinking big is cool.*
Straightforwardness is cool.	*The unexpected is cool.*
Pandering to the crowd is not cool.	*Missionaries are cool.*
Hypocrisy is not cool.	*Mercenaries are not cool.*

Jeff Bezos understands the Ben Franklin Effect. He knows that having a likeable brand will create loyalty among your customers. Being a likeable company, or even a likeable person for that matter, doesn't happen overnight. It takes a lot of small disciplines practiced consistently over a period of time to truly become likeable. It isn't by coincidence that likeable people seem to always have things go their way and unlikeable people seem to get left behind. Do you feel like you get the benefit of the doubt more often than most people, or do you feel like you are always overlooked? Chances are your Likeability is one of the greatest determining factors for you getting the benefit of the doubt.

THE KEY TO MOST PEOPLE'S NETWORK IS THEIR FAMILY

Family is not an important thing. It's everything. —Michael J. Fox

If their family hates you, you will have an uphill battle that is sometimes impossible to climb. However, if the family loves you, it will be as easy as coasting down a small hill on your bicycle. I'm telling you, knowing someone's family is the ultimate sweet spot! There is no easier way to connect with someone and become more likeable than through their family. Of course, getting to know someone's family is neither convenient nor easy. If there is any way you can get to know their family and make that connection, do it. The return on that investment will be greater than you can imagine.

By connecting with someone's family, you are creating a deeper relationship. Whenever you have the opportunity to meet an important family member of one of your contacts, you should pay extra special attention to that person. Ask them as many questions as you can while displaying respect, showing charisma, and expressing genuine interest. I know for me personally that any contact I have that has a connection with my family is instantly someone I generally trust more and would do a favor for.

A great idea for how to connect with your contact's family is to create a fun event that they can invite their family to. Even if you are single, you can still apply this principle by simply being thoughtful. I once hosted 80 people in Lake Powell,

Utah, one of my favorite places on earth. On that trip we had two houseboats, six jet skis, four boats, a monster firework show, and tons of other games.

My good friend Woody Woodward is a professional personal development speaker. I had Woody come down to Powell to hang out but also spend an hour sharing his great personal development content with everyone. Woody's wife was supposed to come but ended up getting sick. After the trip was over, I sent both of them a thank-you card and gift certificate to Woody's wife. Why would I send the card and gift certificate to Woody's wife? Although she was sick, she was still kind enough to lend her husband to me. Here was her exact text response to me:

Hi Rob, this is Shaylene — Woody's wife. I went to get the mail today and what a fun surprise it was to get your incredibly sweet and amazingly thoughtful card! What a class act you are! I have already been impressed by all Woody has told me about you, but this goes far beyond anything I could have imagined! Please know how touched I am, not only by the gift cards (which I absolutely love!) but that you would even spend the time to write me a thank you! You are honestly too kind! I should be thanking you for entertaining my husband for so long! Woody and I have been amazed by how you handled everything during and after Powell. Your character has truly shown! "Hard work spotlights the character of people: some turn up their sleeves, some turn up their noses, and some don't turn up at all." (Sam Ewing) Thank you for your friendship and goodness and your phenomenal character! Sincerely, Shay.

I personally know that family is an integral part of networking. I have tried to get out of several functions, but if the wife really wants to go, then I am always going. If someone wants to make sure they are associated with me, just become good friends with my wife.

The Taker

Meet Jake the Taker, Jake the Unlikeable, and Jake the Jerk; doesn't matter what you call him, for they are all accurate. Before you judge me for exaggerating, you have to read this story. For three years I worked with a company where I was fortunate to have much success. There was another very successful guy there named Jake. Every time I tried to learn from Jake or work with him, he would say, "No offense, but I don't see how this would benefit me." I thought

I brought a different outlook and age group that would add value. He had a scarcity mentality in his approach to the company. He always wanted secret meetings with other successful salespeople. He would even kick out those who weren't part of his team if they somehow showed up at one of his trainings. He exuded the persona of an unlikeable person. He was unwilling to build a relationship by offering advice, sharing ideas, or simply having a nice conversation. He had no interest in depositing his knowledge anywhere but his own business. Trust is like a bank account. You can make withdrawals and deposits. If you make too many withdrawals you will be overdrawn on your trust account.

Three years went by and I moved on to another venture. As I was moving on, I got a call from Jake and he proceeded to tell me that as much success as I had my first three years (which was much better than his first three years with that company), I didn't know the right way to have massive success. He told me he could help take my business to another level. He said he had worked out with the company, a way for me to switch to his team if I would just stay with the same company. If you are new to network marketing that's called cross recruiting. They have an opportunity to help you and to profit from you. By switching to his team, I would have abandoned several other individuals but would have helped Jake to profit more. This man had never taken any interest in me or made any "deposits of trusts," such as a few mere conversations or little pieces of advice. Now he was asking to take out a massive withdrawal when nothing was in the bank.

Two years go by and I don't hear a word from Jake. No texts, no phone calls, nothing on social media. Then, out of the blue, I get a voicemail that told me how talented I was and that we need to meet up. I was swamped at the time and, to be honest, I didn't want to respond, but I did. I simply shot him a text that I was busy for the weekend but we could catch up later. I never heard back from Jake. I assume I didn't hear back because it wasn't convenient at his time. He once again had no interest in me. Jake is the definition of a Taker with a scarcity mentality!

I am allergic to people like this. Don't be that person! In this book you will learn from the 'best abundance' mentality and Giver thinkers in the industry. You will become more aware of Takers and more dialed in on how to become the exact opposite. My values are so strong towards being loyal, taking care of others, and providing value that when someone is the complete opposite, I take it more poorly than most. It's a weakness I need to work on.

CHAPTER 2

THE FORMULA TO BECOMING
MORE LIKEABLE

CREATE ALLIES

Holding onto anger is like drinking poison and expecting the other person to die. — Gautama Buddha.

Relationships are complicated, especially when they have to do with money and competition. We all have different strengths or what I joke around about as superpowers. I feel like one of my developed superpowers is maintaining relationships, even when it can be difficult during the tough times! There are times when you are going to butt heads with other people in your personal life and in business. No matter what, you should mend fences. Having ill-will towards another person doesn't help you or them; it is far better to create allies than enemies.

There are some people you never want to work with again. I can't reiterate it enough, when people are at odds with you, they want the world to know. They feel insecure about what you may say and gossip about you. They will spread their version of the story.

Jef Welch said "Cutting others down to make yourself look tall is a misperception of self-growth." Speaking ill of others reflects poorly on your character and actually shows insecurity.

I pride myself on not burning bridges. I try very hard to communicate things properly to maintain great relationships. I will even go out of my way when there is a miscommunication to ensure that everything is good, but sometimes, because I try so hard, I get stubborn when I don't feel that the effort is recipro-cated. Sometimes I let my stubbornness get the best of me and just give up.

There is rarely a good reason to burn bridges. It is ok to disagree with some-one, but burning a bridge is not wise because it hurts both parties tremendous-ly. We've all heard this saying, and I believe it: if you have a good experience, you tell three people, but if you have a bad experience, you tell twenty. Burnt bridges spread like wildfire and very soon both parties get more upset at each other, causing more backbiting. It is a vicious cycle and no one wins! Although I feel this is a practice I am strong in, I am nowhere near Brian McMullen's level.

Brian is one of the top earners in the entire industry. I have been around Brian when he is mad or frustrated with another person. I have seen him in big fights, but he has found a way to make peace and find common ground every single time. Every time I have had a disagreement or miscommunication with a mutual contact of Brian's, he always goes out of his way to make the peace. He does so without me even asking him because he understands the principle of creating allies rather than enemies. He always drops his pride and thinks with a rich person's mentality.

Being rich or being poor has very little to do with wealth. It has a much deeper meaning. Rich people think long-term, whereas poor people think short-term. You may think that I am talking about money, but that mentality relates to everything: relationships, spirituality, money, physicality, literally everything! Bravado and boldness is outdated and old. Nowadays, thanks in large part to social media, being likeable is one of the modern ways to be successful.

You never want to burn a bridge that you
may want to cross in the future!
Always stay in touch and keep friendships
going regardless of where you are both
at now, because you never know what the
future holds in life.
People want to do business with
people that they can respect and trust
to do the right thing! — Craig Kotter

Likeability Rule #1: **BE POSITIVE**

Smile—SMILING IS YOUR BEST WEAPON!! And remember, your weapons are your superpowers. Smiling can be one of your greatest assets in networking. It makes others feel more comfortable; it makes you more likable and you appear more secure with yourself. You instantly become a more attractive person. Smiling takes very little effort and it costs you absolutely nothing. I learned from a Tony Robbins seminar that by showing a positive emotion (even when you don't feel that way), you scientifically become happier. Actions precede emotions. You have to learn to smile more!

I recently met up with a top speaker and author, and I was enthusiastic about picking his brain. As this top speaker entered the room, something was off. The conversation felt off. Then it hit me. I couldn't get past his lack of smiling. I know, I know! It sounds so dumb, but try having a good conversation with someone who won't crack a smile. It never goes well. It is simply hard to have conversations with people who rarely smile, regardless of who you are, even if you are not a top speaker or author.

The next time you are out with a group of people that you don't know, I want you to try this. Look around at their facial expressions, and I want you to guess— just based on looking at them—who is friendly and who isn't. I will bet that those who smile more are the ones you deem as friendly, and those who seem to rarely smile, you deem as not friendly. You can't judge a book by its cover, but you can almost always judge a person by their smile. A great smile frequently used is one of the most powerful ways to become more likeable.

If you're feeling ambitious, you can even try a little experiment. Go print out two pictures of the same person but only have the person smiling in one of the pictures. I bet if you were to show them to two different groups, people would like the picture of the smiling person more than the picture of the person not smiling. It doesn't get any simpler than that!

POSITIVE BODY LANGUAGE

Communication isn't what you say, it's how you are perceived as you say it! Too many people believe that our words do all of the communicating, when that could not be further from the truth. For every sentence you speak, body language accounts for 55%, tone of voice accounts for 38%, and your actual words account for just 7% of the overall message. This isn't to say that words have very little meaning. Words are very important, as they are part of the overall context of your communication. You can't have a great tone and great body language but then nicely speak obscenities.

Instead of going on about body language, I will point out one very critical aspect that isn't mentioned very often: Let their feet do the talking. Think about it. Feet are the one thing that always tell the truth and no one thinks to look at it. When couples touch their feet together, are they happy or angry? They are always happy! You would be able to tell if they were upset at each other if their feet touched and they quickly pulled away.

If your feet are pointed towards someone, that is usually a good sign. If your feet are pointed sideways when talking to someone, you are probably trying to hurry along the conversation and hoping they don't come any closer to you. If your feet are relaxed and not fidgeting, chances are you are enjoying your conversation. If in the middle of your conversation, the person you are talking to turns their feet towards the exit or away from you, chances are they are no longer enjoying the conversation. Those that are socially deficient never see this.

If you ever have kids, tell them you're all going to Disneyland and I can GUARANTEE you that they will have happy feet! They will start dancing around excitedly and the rest of their body will follow. On the contrary, if you are holding a kid captive at the dinner table when he wants to go and play with his friends, his feet are probably sideways and ready to hop off his chair at a moment's notice.

Those with positive body language always increase their Likeability. As mentioned earlier some studies suggest that only 7 percent of our judgments are based on WHAT PEOPLE ACTUALLY SAY! Right or wrong, we are judging everyone on every little movement. By adjusting the way we move, dress, stand, and interact we can make encounters with others go much easier and smoother. If someone says 'I really appreciate you' but then doesn't make eye contact or smile during that entire conversation you will probably think there is something wrong with them. If someone tells you how much they appreciate you but are on their cell phones the entire time, you won't feel fully appreciated. If someone is slouched and yawning and tells you that they appreciate you, you will probably feel like something is off. Whereas, if you are constantly smiling (but don't be the weirdo who overdoes the smile), making great eye contact and maintaining good posture, your message of appreciation will be received positively.

POSITIVE ATTITUDE

Everyone loves to be around that happy, fun, charismatic person. I'm sure that as you are reading this, you are probably starting to think of the person that always finds the good in everything. This person probably often talks highly of other people. Their enthusiasm and positivity is contagious. The opposite is also true; a person's negativity can also be contagious. There have been times in my life where I am in a fun and happy environment and then someone walks into the scene and the mood is instantly deflated.

We have so much power in how we influence others. Our vibes and our attitudes radiate off of us and can be felt by other people. I love being around people with a positive vibe because it rubs off on me. Their positivity automatically puts me in a better mood. Yet, I've never met a negative person that is also a likeable person. A huge part of increasing your Likeability factor is just deciding to stay positive.

Maintaining a positive attitude will attract other positive people into our lives, and those are the kind of people we want to be around. No one likes to be around the person who is always a victim, talking about how they were wronged or always gossiping about others.

My main mentor and 30+ million dollar earner in network marketing is Lon Wardrop. If it weren't for Lon, I would have never joined the network marketing industry. Many of my teachings are what I call "Lonisms" mixed with my own personal perspective. He deserves so much credit for both his friendship and mentorship. I bring Lon up here in the book because one of his greatest attributes is his attitude. He has a unique ability to always find the positive in every situation. When you ask Lon how he is doing he will respond the same every single time: "having the greatest day of my life." He chooses to always give a great response that affects both his attitude and the attitude of others.

One of the top ways to show you have a positive attitude and to brighten someone else's day is through humor! Well placed and well used humor can make you more relatable. Everyone likes the smart, witty, humorous person. Humor makes others smile and can break the ice very quickly. Make the decision that you will maintain a positive attitude to increase your Likeability factor, and then stick to it!

Likeability Rule #2: BE INTERESTED

You can make more friends in two months by becoming interested in other people than you can in two years by trying to get other people interested in you. — Dale Carnegie

Talk less and listen more. God gave us two ears and one mouth for a reason. People like people that take a genuine interest in them, and there is no way you can learn what you need to learn about a person if you aren't asking questions and listening to what they say. Franklin Roosevelt, the thirty-second president of the United States, believed that most people were poor listeners, especially when it came to making small talk. Every so often, to prove his point and amuse himself, he would greet houseguests with, "I murdered my grandmother this morning." The usual response was a puzzled, yet polite, nod of approval. The fact that the houseguests would respond with any nod of approval says a lot about most people's lack of listening.

Learning to consciously and properly listen is a skill very few of us practice. Talk half as much as the other person you are having a conversation with. People LOVE to talk about themselves, so ask them specific questions. An example would be complimenting them on something they are wearing and then asking them about it. Relationships are about listening empathetically and not solving problems. Don't interrupt. Give others your fully undivided attention. I could go on and on about this, but I'll keep it simple. Talk less and listen more! One of the best ways to show someone respect is to simply listen. Great listeners are likeable. Masa Cemazar and Miguel Montero have made millions in the network marketing industry. Despite all of their experience, money and achievements what impressed me most is their ability to listen. The first time I met both Masa and Miguel, they constantly asked questions and were genuinely interested. Later that same day we went to lunch and they continued to ask questions listening attentively. It wasn't until much later in the day I learned that they were making a million dollars a year. It was one of those moments where I realized I had done an incredible job talking about myself but not a very good job at asking questions. Listen attentively. Listen without the goal of responding or solving problems. Listen to understand the other person.

Sincere Compliments

Want to know a great way to get on someone's good side? Give out compliments! Who doesn't like compliments? Everyone loves receiving them. We all know that one person who is always complimentary. They make you feel good about yourself and you want to be around them more. For some people, compliments come naturally, but for most, they don't. Practice giving three compliments a day to others. If you are feeling bold, go for ten compliments a day. As you get better at it, you will no longer have to think about it. It will become a habit that serves you well. The best part about complimenting others is that it will actually make you happier! The only other tip I would give you is to make sure that your compliments are sincere. Those who give sincere compliments often, are more likeable.

My good friend, Alexander Strate, who helped me write this book, is one of the best people I know at this. He is always smiling and giving out real, sincere compliments. I've seen him pull people away from a group, even just for a moment, to let them know that he appreciates them. This takes less than ten seconds, but I bet you the other person never forgets how Alexander made them feel. Most people never get compliments, so one of the easiest ways to connect with someone is to give a sincere compliment.

I talked to Alexander about how he is really good at giving compliments. His response? "Wow Rob, thank you so much, I appreciate you noticing, not many people would go out of their way to tell me that, I really appreciate that about you." Even when he was saying thank you, he found a way to slide a compliment in because that is who he has become. He no longer has to think about it. Complimenting others is an automatic reaction for him. Alexander has that positive, contagious vibe, and it all starts with his smile and his compliments, usually without even noticing that he is doing it! I can guarantee you if you find ways to consciously give more compliments, it will start to improve the relationships around you and you will live a more positive lifestyle.

Remember Their Name

Your name is the most important word in any language. Don't forget a person's name! Repeat it three times in your head. Associate it with something that will make it memorable. A common saying people like to use is "I'm just bad with names." That is an excuse. What they are really saying is that they don't care enough to remember, or that people are not important enough for them to remember their name.

It's not easy to remember people's names. I have met people who can memorize numerous names in a room without any issues, and I have met people who can't remember a single name at all. If you have a hard time remembering names, make a conscious effort to remember just ONE person's name! Look at Rebecca. Then in your head, say 'Rebecca' over and over again. Then sing it in your head by turning her name into a song. Use her name when you talk to her. Do whatever you have to do to remember it, and once you have one name down, then move on to the next one!

Remembering names when meeting people will take extra focus and listening skills. It will take sincerity. Remembering someone's name can be a great way to make them feel important and relevant. If you make a genuine effort to remember someone's name, I KNOW you can do it. I can promise you they will definitely like you more for simply remembering their name.

PUT YOUR PHONES AWAY

Wherever you are, be all there! — Jim Elliott

GUILTY! I'm not going to pretend to be the golden child here, I do this too! I am guilty, in comfortable friend settings, of having my phone out too much. I don't do this as much in settings with those who I don't know extremely well. My wife reminds me to get rid of my phone in social settings by simply giving me "the look." The one where the eyebrows rise and she glances at the phone and then at me. Even though she looks so attractive when she gives me "the look," I know better and put my phone away.

This principle applies to much more than phones. Be in the moment. If you are at church, be at church. If you are with your family, then be with your family. If you are at a funeral or wedding, then be there! Don't be the annoying person who is always distracted. No one likes that person, no one respects that person, and no one listens to that person. There is a time and place to push your ideas or agenda. Your goal is to be present wherever you are and to become a professional at connecting with others.

Wherever you are, be ALL there! Put your cell phone away when you are in a meeting. If you have to check your phone, take the time and courtesy to tell the other individual why so that they know you respect and value them. Don't be socially clueless! Texting or checking a phone a lot during a conversation is the ultimate slap in the face.

Here are some strategies to stay engaged in the moment rather than distracted by your phone. Remember to smile. I know I've mentioned that you should smile several times now, but it is Likability Rule #1 for a reason! Make good solid eye contact. In groups, don't just talk to one person. Make sure you switch off making contact with the entire group. Remember many times the other people in the meeting have a ton of influence with the individual you are focusing on, so make everyone feel important. I know you may have one person that you are focusing on in a conversation, but by only looking at that person you will make the others feel unimportant.

Putting your phones away and learning to be in the moment will greatly increase your LIKEABILITY. Cell phones bring us much closer to those who are far from us, but they take us away from those who are sitting right next to us.

Likeability Rule #3: BE REAL
FIND COMMONALITIES

People like people who like them. Think about it. Is there anyone you like who hates you? People also like people who are like them. Finding commonalities will go a long way in establishing instantaneous Credibility with the other person. My friend and expert network marketer Rachael Davenport likes to call this the "Me Too" game. Expert networkers will keep asking questions until they find something that enables them to say "Me Too!"

If you are a Denver Broncos fan wearing a Broncos jersey in public, and you just so happen to run into someone else that is also wearing a Broncos jersey, the world freezes. You make eye contact with this person, and then they see you as well. As you walk by each other heading in opposite directions, you give that person the slightest of nods, which is reciprocated by a grin and a nod. You have no idea who that person is, or their background, and you'll probably never see them again, but if you are a guy, you just established a bromance with a total stranger because of your mutual interest in the Broncos. (Note; many women are bigger football fans than men. This is just an analogy.)

Now, there are other ways to find commonalities besides just wearing sports jerseys in public. You may have the same taste in music, or love a certain restaurant, or there may be a common activity that you two could discuss and relate to. Whatever the case, do your best to instantly establish some commonalities and make that connection! Ask questions. Questions give the answers. Through questions you can find commonalities. Find some way to relate to others, and you will build both your trust and your Likeability factor.

Show Empathy

"YOU'RE FIRED!" Donald Trump made this phrase popular on his show "The Apprentice." The phrase itself is a little harsh and was created to stir up ratings. There is a simple solution to giving others bad news or hearing bad news from others. Now, this simple solution would have made the ratings plummet on "The Apprentice," but we don't want to live in a reality TV show or game show, we want to avoid drama! This solution is so simple, yet if you apply it, you will instantly come across as more empathetic and be more likeable to those around you. It is something you can apply to your life right away and start generating stronger relationships almost instantly. Out of all the Likeability rules, I think that this one has to be the easiest to apply if you just do this one thing. Are you ready to hear what it is?

Whenever you are delivering bad news, just say "Sorry." That's all!

What if you aren't sorry? Finds ways to be sorry. I'm sure if the relationship really means enough to you, you'll find a way to make it happen. Even if someone has upset you or even if it is completely their fault, put yourself in their shoes. If it is something negative that will affect this individual and that sucks for them, you should feel some sort of empathy. No one should truly enjoy someone else's pain, even if it is deserved.

When I get a text with a question that I have no clue how to answer, I always send out a simple text and follow it with, "I'm sorry." If someone leaves your organization in network marketing and you couldn't stand working with them, find a way to feel sorry. Maybe you feel sorry for the other person because they weren't successful or you couldn't connect with them better. Honestly, it doesn't matter. Empathy is powerful and it goes a long way.

Just because I feel sorry for something or someone doesn't mean that I change my decision. My main point is that it never hurts to be blunt in an empathetic way. If it can't hurt, then why not practice being sorry and understanding. Understand where they are coming from and then do what you need to do. The excuse, "I am just blunt" is a justification that someone is either bad at communicating or simply doesn't care enough. I am blunt, but I always do my best to understand their side. Be bluntly empathetic.

Empathy can be used in so many ways to have more influence. If you are dealing with people in any sort of a service industry, like airlines, hotels, or food industries, you know that these businesses deal with a lot of whiners. By simply being empathetic with them for being busy, for having a tough job, or anything like that, you will dramatically increase your chances of getting more of what you want. People are more inclined to help those who understand them than those who yell at them. Empathetic people are simply more likeable and likeable people tend to have things go their way.

If you still aren't convinced, let's look at a real-life example that we can all relate to. We all have a little road rage in us. If you don't, then you aren't human. Imagine you are in hurry, racing through town in your car, and all of the sudden someone pulls out in front of you. They cut you off big time and, to make matters worse, they don't even try to make up for it by putting their foot on the pedal! At this point you probably have several choice words in mind or maybe even out loud for this individual. As you pull up next to them at a red light, they mouth to you how sorry they are over and over. You also notice they are a senior citizen that just didn't see you. Their facial expression is sincere and you can tell they are actually sorry. Now you may still be bothered. You may still be mouthing a few choice words but more than likely you are instantly not as mad at this individual simply because they said they were sorry. You probably even wave back and mouth back 'it's ok.'

Rachel Jackson has built a great organization by maximizing her strengths. Rachel is great with people. She shines in one-on-one situations because she has mastered showing empathy for others. She mirrors how they are feeling. She understands where they are coming from. Then, she creates goals that are all about them and their current situation. She then shares all of her struggles in network marketing, but follows with many teaching lessons from those struggles. Rachel then casts a massive vision on how the struggles are part of the journey to success. Her balance of understanding others all while giving them unique perspective on success have helped propel her business. She does an incredible job of empowering everyone in her organization and does so by starting with strong empathy.

Learn to show empathy, even in the most difficult circumstances, and you will create a strong connection and increase your Likeability.

Be Authentic & Genuine

John Huntsman Sr. gave up about $200 million because of a handshake! There are few people that have more integrity than John Huntsman. When he was in the early days of his business, he had to sell some of it to generate some cash flow. In one deal, he agreed to sell 40 percent of his company for $53 million. This deal experienced great delays between the handshake, the agreement, and when the deal was actually completed. During this delay, the company experienced a huge burst of growth. When the time came for the payment, that original 40 percent agreement was now worth about $250 million. Mr. Huntsman could have re-worked the deal in order to get $197 million more, since the handshake with his partner was not legally binding. Instead, he kept his word, and told his partner, "I shook your hand. I made an agreement. The price will be $53 million. That's what we agreed to months ago."

Mr. Huntsman could have thrown his integrity aside to get almost $200 million more, but his integrity with that handshake was worth more than that to him. Once your integrity is ruined, it is practically impossible to get back. While money is important, and it is hard to survive without it, your integrity is worth even more.

Your authenticity is your greatest weapon. Build trust and Credibility by communicating the truth. Do not exaggerate! The worst thing you can do is embellish and tell people what they want to hear rather than the truth. I don't care if you do real estate, work for minimum wage, are in network marketing, or are unemployed, once your trust is gone, it is nearly impossible to gain it back. Network marketing is about building partnerships. You can only build partnerships through trust, and you can only build trust through honesty. "If you don't tell the truth, your downline may be friendly to you—but they probably won't follow you." said Tim Sales.

What good is a partnership if one of the partners is lying to the other? Whether it's a blatant lie, or a slight exaggeration, a lie is a lie. I would much rather under-promise and over-deliver, rather than over-promise and under-deliver.

Network marketing has the potential to make all your wildest dreams come true, or it could do the exact opposite. One of my favorite topics is "Dreaming big versus managing expectations." I had to learn through trial and error. When I first started in this industry, I was all about dreaming big; I fed into the hype and I loved it. I fed into selling hype and seeing it as normal. The problem with selling hype is that everything is exaggerated so much that it doesn't set the right expectations. It sets a warped sense of what the norm is. When your team goes through a trial or struggle they are often unprepared for it because they were only prepared for the best-case scenario.

After seeing the issues that came with pitching hype, I shifted to the opposite side; I gave everyone the cold hard facts of how hard this industry is without empowering them to be better. I wanted them to understand how hard this was going to be before they got started. By going the opposite way, I wasn't seeing others for their best. I was seeing them all for just being average. I wasn't being a good leader and wasn't inspiring anyone to be the best version of themselves.

Network marketing leader Brandon Hayes says it best, "Don't look for average people. Average people do nothing. Don't be average."

As you can see, neither way worked. One was way too much hype, and the other was way too discouraging. I wasn't seeing the best in people and letting them dream. I had to learn to merge the two sides together. I did that by simply giving both the dream along with the averages. This gave people the opportunity to dream big but also gave them a reality check in case they didn't achieve those dreams.

Be an authentic person who isn't afraid to show some weaknesses. To be likeable, you don't need to be perfect. In fact, many will love you because of your imperfections because they will be able to relate better with you. I always make sure to share all of the weaknesses that I have overcome, with my audiences, as well as maybe something that I am working on. Be real! Authentic and genuine trustworthy people are likeable. "When you have the courage show people glimpses of your humanity; then what they get is you." — Richard Bliss Brooke, author of the bestselling Network Marketing book *The Four Year Career.*[®]

Be careful with how you communicate your authenticity. Sometimes we try to be authentic, but it backfires on us because we try too hard, too fast. If you haven't yet developed a relationship of trust you might have the opposite effect of what you had hoped for. Phrases like, "Let me know how I can serve you" and "How can I help you?" are not to be used too soon or too freely. If it is used before you actually know someone, others will think your intentions aren't genuine. That sounds crazy but remember people are skeptical. They will think, "What's the catch? What's your hidden agenda? You don't know me well enough to help me, you weirdo."

Todd Falcone is brutally honest. Follow him on Facebook or go look up some of the trainings he has given. He is not only an industry legend, but he is also one of the best speakers/trainers in the entire industry. As you follow him on social media you know instantly that he is authentic and that he will tell you exactly what he is thinking. It doesn't matter if you know him or not, you know by watching his content that he is real and authentic. It is easy to trust those who give no fluff, no exaggerations, and are just real with you. People like that seem to be a dying breed and are so refreshing to encounter.

Increasing your authenticity will help you be more successful in all aspects of your life. It is one of the key success principles that isn't given enough credit and is rarely talked about. If you practice what I just taught you about becoming more likeable, you will have plenty to work on in your journey to become a more likeable person. Trust me, it's worth it!

THE DATING GAME

*Make new friends, but keep the old. Those are
silver, these are gold.* — Joseph Parry

The point of The Likeability Factor is to make new friends and associations, but you can't do that if you don't meet new people. Think of networking like the dating game. When you are single and looking to meet someone, you would be open to as many opportunities as possible that could lead you to hopefully meet "The One." You would be the most social version of you. You'd be absolutely more likely to go to social events outside your comfort zone to meet new people whenever you could! Tailgating before the football game? You're in! A neighborhood get-together where you barely know anyone? Maybe not normally, but this isn't normally. In networking, it should be just like the dating game. When you understand the real currency of networking, you will make time to find opportunities to meet others and practice your likeability with them.

Meeting new people can go a lot of different ways. You can either treat the new people you meet with the same respect as someone you have a one-night stand with, or you can treat them like you are looking for a long-term stable relationship. Now, I'm no expert on one-night stands. I don't have any personal experience, but I do have an amazing wife that I am in a happy long-term relationship with. I know that if I had treated my wife poorly when we first met, or if I didn't try to get to know her better, that we would not be in the position we are today. If someone is feeling like they are being used, they will be turned OFF, and very quickly!

Just as it is important to treat people respectfully when you meet them, it is also important you are meeting the right kind of people. There are tons of different ways to meet new people. The kind of people that you will meet will be dependent upon the kind of event or place you go to. Try:

- Religious Events
- Exercise Classes
- Hobby Clubs
- Art Classes
- Coffee Shops
- Animal Parks
- Conferences
- Retreats
- Ethnic or Gender-Based Clubs

- Local Colleges or Universities
- Social Media
- Alumni Events
- Trade Shows
- Music Events
- Online Forums
- Blogging
- Toastmasters
- Volunteer Work

When you purposefully network, you are going to surround yourself with the people that you choose, not the ones that just happen to end up around you. A good network being created is like a merger of two good companies. It allows you to accentuate your strengths and hide your weaknesses. What was a weakness of yours may be a strength of your network, and you are now able to reach farther than you previously would have been able to because of your expanded network. Get out there and purposefully network; you have nothing to lose and a whole network to gain! Although this book focuses on how to network, I have a free eBook that will teach you how to take one person and turn them into thousands. This technique will help you to never run out contacts. In network marketing we call that strategy taprooting. This eBook is focused on the techniques to taprooting. Go to www.robsperry.com/blueprint/ for the free download.

CHAPTER 3

THE LAW OF
CREDIBILITY

LAW #2

*Success is not to be pursued; it is to be attracted
by the person you become.* — Jim Rohn

Would you travel hundreds of miles in all kinds of horrible weather conditions, day and night, week after week, just to keep a promise you really didn't want to make in the first place?

Frodo Baggins in the *Lord of the Rings* is the definition of Credibility. While living a calm and peaceful life in his grassy hometown called "The Shire," a wizard friend named Gandalf came to visit one day. Gandalf bluntly shared that Frodo's world as he knew it was going to come to an end unless Frodo traveled across the land, hundreds of miles, and threw a tiny little ring into a very specific volcano. Easy enough, right?

Now, Frodo was not in good shape or equipped for the job, but he agreed to do it anyway (I guess it's hard to say no to a wizard!). Frodo and his partners took off trekking across the land in rain and snow, the scorching sun, through swamps and spiders, and up sharp, treacherous mountain sides. Finally, when Frodo did make it to the specific volcano, he was so exhausted from his journey that he almost died before finally throwing the ring into it and saving the world.

Now, if I need something done, and my friend Frodo says he will help me make it happen, do you think I will have any doubt that Frodo would help get the job done? No! He built his Credibility by saying he was going to do something and then doing WHATEVER IT TOOK to get the job done.

The Credibility you build as an individual is a key point to your overall networking success. I am going to teach you to do what Frodo did, except without the whole near-death experience part (if that's ok with you, of course). If you don't put the practices I am about to teach you to good use, you are going to end up really pissing off your grandma.

WARNING HIGHLY SARCASTIC. There is a secret formula that will help you piss off your grandma, and join the all-exclusive NFL (No Friends League) Hall of Fame and become the most annoying neighbor your community has ever seen. This training is not limited to just those topics. I will also give you tips on how to get instantly blocked on social media and even become an orphan. Buckle up, because it's about to get wild!

Tip #1: *Pesky Persistence*. Call your friends and family everyday about your opportunity. When they say no, they obviously must not understand, so you should start calling three times a day. Pesky Persistence is the key to losing friends and not influencing people.

Tip #2: *Overhype*. If you think someone can make $500 a month always add on two more zeros. Always over promise. Besides, doesn't $50,000 a month sound way more intriguing than $500 a month? Follow this strategy and your neighbors are guaranteed to hate you.

Tip #3: *Sell Sell Sell*. Mansion Monday, Gold Watch Wednesday, and Ferrari Friday are my three favorite days of the week. Why only hype up how much money you can make? Promise more than money. Oversell the dream because who doesn't like a cocky salesperson?

Tip #4: *The Cure All*. If you are truly committed to the NFL, you will sell a wild, crazy, over-the-top story about how you "aren't supposed to make claims… but your friend's babysitter's dog's cousin's illness was cured by your product." Everyone hates an outrageous lie that is sure to be investigated by legal authorities, so save this for your most special contacts ONLY.

Tip #5: *Social Media*. Please post five times a day MINIMUM about what an idiot everyone else is for not being in your company while you talk about how great your business is. Be very offensive and belittling, letting them know how truly dumb they are and how brilliant, rich, and especially blessed you are.

I can guarantee that these tips will drastically improve your odds for pissing off your grandma, joining the all-exclusive No Friends League Hall of Fame, and becoming the most annoying neighbor your community has ever seen. I can also promise very confidently that your odds will also increase on getting in- stantly blocked on social media and even becoming a disowned orphan. I could go on and on about these principles, but if you truly want a great laugh as well as great insight on what to do, go buy the book *Don't Be "That Guy" in Network Marketing* by Adam and Michelle Carey. However, if you want to read how NOT to do these things, read on.

CREATE YOUR GREATNESS

You were born with potential.
You were born with goodness and trust.
You were born with ideals and dreams.
You were born with greatness.
You were born with wings.
You are not meant for crawling, so don't.
You have wings.
Learn to use them and fly. — Rumi

Once you have had success, it will make it easier (not easy) to have success again.

Now, I know it may be tough, and at times it may seem impossible. However, you must do whatever it takes to become great at something. You must create credibility. I don't care what it is. Honestly, it could be that you're the best bowler in the state, or maybe you are the most consistent person at the gym. People love being around greatness.

Look at all of the famous celebrities and athletes who don't have the best personal lives, but people still gravitate towards them because of their greatness. I know there are a lot of people who don't like Floyd Mayweather, myself included, but you can't help but notice him when you see him in person and be like, "Holy cow, that's Floyd Mayweather." Being great at something will make networking so much easier.

I know it isn't easy, but if you don't have that story yet, you need to figure out what you are going to be great at! It will bring you Credibility in everything that you do. Go crush one thing to prove to yourself that you are capable of greatness.

Network Marketing is a business. We don't promise fortune or fame
with NO work. This isn't "NOT-work Marketing." It's Net-work marketing.
There is work involved. Know that from the start. — Tara Wilson

The principles of success are the same in everything you do. The technique will be different, but the principles for success are universal. Whether you are in school, sports, music, acting, or the business world, you will have to abide by the exact same principles of success. These principles include hard work, taking responsibility, discipline, commitment and perseverance. What you don't see on this list is the word "talent." Interesting isn't it? When we talk about Credibility, we aren't talking about the most talented individual on the team. We are talking about the person that PROVES their talent and that's what true Credibility looks like. A great book on this is called *Talent is Overrated* by Geoffrey Colvin. Network marketing Consultant Christopher Hussey says, "You must take one small step at a time as you build your empire and achieve those long-term goals. Many people fail to truly build their network marketing business because they are looking too far ahead, and they fail to take the daily actions required to keep their business growing."

As you learn these success principles, you will learn how you can apply them to everything. As you succeed, you will also build trust in yourself. Your confidence will grow in your ability to have success in anything you do. Your greatest skills will attract your greatest contacts. I am a tennis player. I met my business partner Lance Conrad through the tennis club. Look through your best contacts, and I will bet that most of them were developed from what you do best. Stop and really think about that last sentence. Think about your very best contacts. Did some or many of them come from what you do best?

If you're like most people, you are on the fast track to getting a Bachelor's Degree in Wasting Time, and that's not good! Figure out your time wasters. You can't create greatness without eliminating your distractions.

What are those top distractions that have no true return on your investment? The first thing that most people think of is the TV. Don't waste time on TV! There is an opportunity cost involved. You are not only paying monthly for it, but you are also wasting time watching it when you could be doing something to build your future. Imagine eliminating two hours of TV a day. That's 14 hours a week. That's 56 hours a month, or over two full days that you get back and can be productive with. You have to give up what you like to earn what you love.

Giving up what you like to earn what you love is one of the hardest success principles for people to truly understand. My first six months in network marketing, I completely eliminated TV. I am an avid tennis fan, and I missed all of the US Open in 2008 and the entire epic Summer Olympics with Michael Phelps setting records. I didn't watch even one minute of TV during those six months because I needed to create greatness, and I did.

Now that I have created a story, I am still disciplined on the amount of TV I watch, but at 10 p.m. I will watch a show with my wife that is on either Netflix or DVR. On the main floor of my house, there is no TV anywhere in the kitchen or living room area. I stopped watching the NFL, with the exception of some huge games, and now I have almost completely quit watching tennis. I watch my favorite NBA and college football team whenever I can, but I have drastically gotten rid of so many distractions. I liked what I gave up, but I love what I have earned.

Some people would say what I did (or currently still do) is painful. I would say it has helped to create my dream lifestyle. The radio or listening to music can also be a time waster. I traded in music for audio books. When I am at the gym for an hour, I now listen to books to maximize my time. If this scares you, chill out! You have to decide what are your outlets and what are your distractions. My outlet is movies. I love movies. Movies inspire me. For others, their inspiration or outlet happens to be music. You need to figure out what are your distractions.

Another major distraction is our phone. According to Simon Chan, founder of MLM Nation, "We have tons of distractions and Time Thieves that steal our time and thus steal our money every day and one of the worst Time Thieves is the cell phone!" I won't go into detail, as we all know how distracting a phone can be. The question is what are you willing to give up to give you more time to create the life that you can own? Discipline isn't to take away from what you want in life. Discipline is there to give you everything you really want in life. Everything has a price. Discipline in the right habits helps you earn what you want. Distractions are everyone's struggle. Distractions are a mirage that prevent you from achieving everything you desire. Discipline may seem to be an enemy that you never want to embrace, but in reality discipline is your true ally. Whitney Husband is one of the world's most successful network marketers. She is also a young mother of 2 kids. She says to ask yourself this, "is what I am doing right now really working." I think this is relevant because many times we think we are working but we are wasting time with distractions. Whitney goes on to say that social media is very powerful but many times we scroll through Facebook way too often. Later on in this book I will teach you more on how to properly use social media.

Things which matter most must never be at the mercy of things which matter least. —Johann Wolfgang von Goethe

The Law of Credibility Comes
Through Creating That Greatness

In my opinion, the following story illustrates one of the greatest social experiments. A man stood at a Metro station in Washington, DC, playing the violin. He played six Bach pieces for about 45 minutes. During that time, it was calculated that 1,100 people went through the station, most of whom were on their way to work.

Three minutes went by, and a middle-aged man noticed there was a musician playing. He slowed his pace and stopped for a few seconds, and then hurried along. A few minutes later, someone leaned against the wall to listen to him, but the man looked at his watch and started to walk again. Clearly, he was late for work. During the entire 45 minutes, only six people stopped and stayed for any length of time. About 20 gave him money but continued to walk. He collected a paltry $32. When he finished playing and silence took over, no one noticed. No one applauded, nor was there any recognition.

The violinist was Joshua Bell, and he's considered to be one of the best musicians in the world. He had just played one of the most intricate pieces ever written, on a Stradivarius violin worth $3.5 million dollars. Two days before he played in the subway, Joshua sold out at a theater in Boston where the cheap seats were $100 each. Due to his extreme talent, Joshua often charges upwards of $1,000 per minute. Go look up Joshua Bell on Google. He is the real deal!

This endeavor was made possible by a "social experiment" by the *Washington Post*.

The lesson I want to point out is the Law of Credibility. Credibility is very difficult to earn but greatly amplifies everything you say or do once it is earned. If you receive incredible advice from a non-successful friend vs the exact same word for word advice from Warren Buffett, would it be received differently? The Law of Credibility had this same effect on Joseph Bell. When he was properly edified and promoted at a Boston theater, cheap seats sold for $100. The next day, when no one knows who he was, there was very little interest.

Joshua Bell wasn't the only superstar to garner little interest at one point. Luke Hessler was an average college student. He was a great guy who was young and had no experience or Credibility for building a business. What Luke did have, however, was determination, crazy enthusiasm, and a strong work ethic. Luke went out and did everything he possibly could to create a story. He achieved success in a network marketing company by working hard and pushing through those fears we all have. Luke went from being considered the popular kid on a big college campus to the crazy, weird kid.

At first, network marketing was social suicide. Luke's friends weren't interested in creating a business. They were enjoying the college scene and interested in partying. Despite his struggles, Luke pushed through and created greatness once, which gave him Credibility and amplified his efforts. Now he is absolutely crushing it. Luke is currently known as one of the top millennial network marketers in the world.

It isn't easy earning Credibility. Luke struggled his first few months in network marketing, but he was determined to do whatever it took, for however long it took. It will take everything you have, but once you create it, you will see that it will positively amplify everything else you do. If you say the same thing or even something more profound than Warren Buffett, it won't have anywhere close to the same effect. Warren Buffett has created the story. He has created that Credibility. Do whatever it takes to become great. Being good isn't good enough. As Jim Collins says, "Good is the enemy of great."

You need to breakthrough and create greatness once, just once! That is Credibility. Once you have proven it to yourself, you know you can do it again, and again, and again! There will be nothing stopping you from creating the success you need that will fit perfectly into your all-powerful story. Your story starts from creating that success and continues endlessly as your greatness evolves.

And where I excel is ridiculous, sickening, work ethic. You know,
while the other guy's sleeping? I'm working. —Will Smith

THE POWER OF STORYTELLING

Gary Vaynerchuk says that "storytelling is by far the most underrated skill in business." Your story of yourself will attract or repel others. We all have tragedies and victories. What's your version of your story? Did you learn and grow or did you blame?

They say that facts tell and stories sell, so let me tell you a quick story about my friend Ty Bennett. Ty realized just how much power there was in storytelling, so he wrote a book called just that: *The Power of Storytelling*. In it, he outlines how to tell your story. There is so much content throughout the book, but one huge insight I took away from his book was to always tell your story like you are telling it the first time. You need to have that same high energy and passion each time you tell your story. It doesn't matter if it's your fourth time or your four thousandth time. The person listening to your story might miss that one key thing they are looking for if you are not engaging enough and telling your story with enthusiasm.

How to Evolve into a Conqueror

When I helped to create a brand new initiative for a company that had $3 billion in lifetime sales, it was quite the project. The parent company was struggling and was looking for a rebrand, so Lance Conrad, Brandon Carter, and I rebranded them in the United States with new products, culture, name, demographic, and systems. A year into the rebrand, we had turned a corner, and the company finally started having more distributors joining than falling out for the first time in five years.

Unfortunately, it wasn't enough as the parent company had leveraged themselves with a $100 million+ loan. A venture capitalist had taken control of the company and wanted out. They wanted to sell the company.

At this point, I had a choice to make. I could be victim and create a story about how I got screwed over by the parent company. I could blame the venture capitalists, or I could focus on all of the positives and think of what solutions there were to this situation. I scrambled together two different potential buyers. One of these two bought the company and, according to most experts, the largest merger in the history of the industry was created. Not only was the largest merger created, but it all happened from first contact to acquisition within five days. Had I told myself a victim story and not taken a proactive approach, there is a good chance that the company would have been merged with an unsuited buyer. Instead of focusing on the problem, I focused on solutions and was a Conqueror.

The way you tell your story will perfectly reflect what kind of person you are. Do yourself a favor and make your story a great one, every single time. For example, did you watch one of Kobe Bryant's most embarrassing games of his entire career? Kobe Bryant, as an 18-year-old rookie in the NBA, shot 4 horrific air balls at the end of a playoff game to the Utah Jazz. After the game Bryant said "I had some good looks. I just didn't hit the shots." He didn't make excuses and later went on to tell reporters that he will keep taking those shots. As you know, Kobe became one of the best players under pressure in NBA history helping the Lakers win five championships. He didn't let those shots define him or his career. He took control of his story and it reflected who he was and who he became.

Just as Kobe Bryant didn't allow a bad game to diminish his confidence, Byron Belka didn't allow a potentially harmful, negative experience to weaken his resolve. Byron is a bright success story of network marketing and one of most well-respected names in the industry. He entered into the network marketing world in the early 2000s. It started as a small favor to a friend that quickly grew into something much deeper. Very soon, after he had established his business, an opportunity presented itself and he moved his young family from the United States to Europe. However, somewhere along the line, he was taken advantage of financially by another leader within the same company. Many of the details after this exchange are of little consequence, only the fact that he continued moving forward with tenacity despite this offense remains important.

He could very well have created a "poor me" attitude, developed bitterness, housed disdain and hate, and written his own victim story. But, that isn't in his character. He simply learned from the experience, and applied the knowledge that he gained into another venture. Since he started network marketing, he has made success a habit, rising through the ranks of virtually every organization he has been a part of, and now is the founder and CEO of his very own network marketing company. He will tell you now that this "bad experience" was the best thing that could have happened to him in his career. Byron was, and is, a conqueror of his circumstance. He turned a negative experience into a learning experience and propelled that into an incredible network marketing career.

I'm going to go a little deeper with you and help you understand this 'Conqueror' mentality from a psychological standpoint by introducing you to the term "Confirmation Bias." The definition of Confirmation Bias, according to Investopedia, is a psychological phenomenon that explains why people tend to seek out information that confirms their existing opinions and overlook or ignore information that refutes their beliefs. This basically means that we will do anything possible to prove ourselves right, even if it means ignoring the obvious right in front of us. Another word for Confirmation Bias that might be a little more psychologically understandable? Stubborn!

Stubbornness is one of the greatest thieves of the Conqueror Mindset. If we could learn to lay down our swords and not pick a fight over every little thing just because we want to prove ourselves right, we would be able to empower ourselves and others so much more! Understanding this principle helps me to always look at things from a Conqueror perspective. I always ask myself the question, "What is the other person's perspective?" This helps me to lay down my sword, see things from the other person's point-of-view, and then I usually give them the benefit of the doubt.

Don't Look At Everyone As A Prospect

I reeked of desperation and repelled others from me because of it. I still remember my first few days, weeks, and even months in network marketing. Every time I saw anyone, anywhere (and I mean anywhere), the only thing I could think was 'how can I get them in my business?' I was obsessed! How much Credibility do you think you are building if every single person you talk to ends up being prospected? Not much!

As soon as I finally fully committed LONG-TERM to network marketing, it gave me perspective. I still had the crazy urgency, focus, determination, and mindset of looking for a reason that everyone should be a part of my business, but something changed.

I developed a relaxed, confident intensity. I started to focus on providing value for others. I started looking at others in terms of how my business would be a fit for them, whereas at the beginning I was looking at how everyone could make me money. I had been looking at the new person as a prospect rather than a partner or even just someone I could help. When you are 100 percent committed, and you start looking at helping everyone, that is when you have arrived for the long-haul. Even if they don't join your business, you are still excited to help them out in any way that you can, because you are now not just a network marketer, you are on a mission to become a master networker.

By not looking at everyone as a prospect, and instead looking at people as human beings with greatness inside of them, Johnnie has become one of those magnetic leaders in network marketing that people just want to be around. When I think of master networkers, I think of my good friend Johnnie Green. Johnnie has the unique ability to connect with everyone. He connects with people from all backgrounds and different walks of life by always seeing the best in others and helping them maximize their potential to achieve more. He is a great example of how to treat others.

If you're in network marketing, then I am sure you know the feeling where you believe you are doing everything right yet nothing is working at all! By doing everything right I mean you are constantly inviting new people to look at your business and try your products or services. You are struggling to get anyone interested. Finally you have someone join your team... only to have them quit one week later! We have all gone through this roller coaster of emotions as network marketers, and being genuine to each other is a huge key to ensuring we keep our chin up and never quit on our journey.

Building Credibility Through Telling Your Story

Marketing is no longer about the stuff that you make,
but about the stories you tell. — Seth Godin

We don't like to brag about ourselves to others. Telling people who you are or what you have done isn't bragging. The biggest key is how you tell them. If I say, "I was considered by far the best recruiter in a multi-billion-dollar company and know more than anyone else," that could come off wrong. Instead why not say, "I was the top recruiter for a billion-dollar company. I got there because I had incredible mentors, that I will forever be grateful for, I outworked everyone, and I was very coachable." Tell your story in a confident, but not cocky, way.

Why is this important? People want to follow a leader. It gives them confidence. Sometimes they don't yet have the confidence in themselves and want to find someone they can follow who has confidence and inspires others to have more. You may ask yourself, "What if I haven't had any success yet?" There are multiple ways to overcome this.

1. You should be able to sell another leader's success in your organization. Leverage their success.
2. I would bet you have been successful in something in your life. Leverage that. When I started network marketing, I leveraged my tennis success and my leader's success. I told everyone how committed and determined I was in tennis and that I would apply that same commitment and discipline to network marketing. I was going to do whatever it takes!
3. If you feel you have no leadership help, nor any success in your life to leverage, then sell your goals.

At the beginning of my network marketing experience, I told people, "I am grateful I have a job, but I want more. I am sick and tired of having no time freedom. I want to travel the world. I want to spend more time with my family and friends. I want to do bigger and better things, so I am going to do whatever it takes to make XX amount of money! I want to reach that goal within two years. It may take me five years or longer, but I am going to do whatever it takes."

Do you hear the confidence I had in what I said? I was not cocky, and I put no one down. Instead, I was 100 percent certain that I was going to make my goals happen, and that's what I was able to show to others. Don't tell people what you do for a living. Tell them the problems you solve. No one cares about what you do. They care about what you can do.

What if they ask me how much money I am making? Every situation is different. If you are someone who is brand-new or relatively new, it is very easy. I would simply say, "Businesses on average take three years to turn a profit. I am building the foundation for my business by learning the skills. I couldn't be more committed and excited about my business. I am going to do whatever it takes to achieve my goals."

Take that principle of how long businesses typically take to turn a profit and intertwine it into your story. For example, if I have been in network marketing for four months and I have made $350, this is how you could respond: "Business is going great. Most business don't turn a profit for three years. I have already made money, learned a ton, and I am working with some very successful mentors." You are also welcome to let them know what you made.

Many times, I even go further to give real life examples. If you had $100,000 in the bank (depending on where interest rates are now) you would make less than $100 a month. If you invest in real estate, it can cost you about 20 percent down and then you hope to cash flow a few hundred dollars. Residual income is hard to come by. I love having a business that gives me the opportunity to build a residual income.

As you learn to tell your story, there are times where you will have to be short! Your story could take about two minutes, or even less. I would learn how to tell your story in 30 seconds, two minutes, five minutes, and ten minutes. As you get more experience, you will eventually develop your story even further, but those are great benchmarks to start.

The 30 Second Story is like your "Elevator Story." You hop on an elevator with another person. You are dressed up very nicely and exude an aura of confidence and positivity, and they look at you and can't help but ask, "Excuse me, but who are you and what do you do?" You only have 30 seconds before the elevator is on your floor. What do you say? Whatever it is, you better make it quick and powerful, and find a way to follow up with this person by getting their contact information!

The Two Minute Story is good for short encounters, or if you are going back and forth asking questions. If you are having a good discussion with someone and the opportunity to tell your story comes up, you don't want to bore them to tears by going on and on for ten minutes; instead, learn to tell your story in two minutes. Find a way to relate to the person, show them why you matter and why you are interesting, and then make sure you are able to keep in touch with them.

The Five Minute Story is a whole new ball game. This story can have a beginning, middle, and end that can be clearly defined. You should definitely spend a good deal of time relating to the person or the audience in the beginning of your story, because if you don't grab their attention right away, you are going to lose them early and they won't hear a word you say! The middle of your story is where you are able to sell yourself. Why do you matter? Why should this person listen to you? What are you looking to accomplish? The end of your story should always be progressive and positive. You should end on an enthusiastic note, looking towards the future with your big goals, incorporating the person or people you are talking to into your goals, or both!

The Ten Minute Story. If your story is this long that means that it's part of some sort of presentation. This is a time where you can let the other person really dream with you. You can bring in testimonials or studies backing up your main points of your story, you can ask the other person rhetorical questions to keep them engaged, and you can really paint the vision for what you want to do with your life.

There is no need to hold back when you know you can share your story for ten minutes. Take the other person along for the ride of your imagination. Your story can inspire and empower others. The best presentations feel like someone isn't selling you. The best presentations are stories being told. Once you can present the business, products, and your story all in a way that works together, you will create an incredible flow that will inspire the masses, and inspiring large groups of people creates massive Credibility.

Set your sights on exactly what you want and what you need. Don't focus on the dollar. Focus on what you need and what you want. You can push yourself to be limitless. There is nothing you won't do when you have that thing you want in mind. Your focus is so powerful. You are unstoppable. — Angel Fletcher

How to Avoid the Awkward Stage

Now, no matter how good you get at telling your story, there are going to be people that reject you. I'm here to tell you that is not a problem! Most of you are familiar with the awkward time for a few days, weeks, or even months when a friend/family member says no to your business. Some people are so scared of this awkward time, they don't join your business for this very reason. You know what I'm talking about, right? I mean, how do you transition from presenting your business and products, being told no, and then going back to the way things were almost like you weren't just mentally slapped in the face?

Sometimes it is awkward! Sometimes it is them being awkward, sometimes it's you, and sometimes it is both of you. You were excited to tell them about your business and then your friend or family member didn't see your business the same way as you. They might've said things that you took as hurtful. You might have offended them in response. Regardless of your specific situation, rest assured there is a simple solution.

It's all about the follow up. I always follow up a rejection from a friend or a family member with a text that says something like this: "Thanks Mike for taking the time to look over our products and business. I really appreciate your opinion and time. Let's go to lunch soon." Or find something that has connected you with this friend/family member and text about it. Joke around if you can find a way to truly show them that you are still friends beyond your differences. I wouldn't just send this text or call them immediately afterwards. I would find an excuse to reach out again within the week. When you reach out, there should be no mention of business, as they have already given you a clear "no" for the time being. Remember, the awkward stage can be a little sensitive, so make sure not to hint at your business at all unless you want to come across as a sleazy salesperson.

THE 100 MILLION DOLLAR QUESTION

What advice would someone give who has made over $100 million? Growing up, my friend Lance Conrad decided he wanted to be successful. One of his best childhood friends came from a very successful family. His friend's Dad was worth over $100 million. Lance wanted to be successful so badly that one day he swallowed his fears, approached him, and asked for advice. He wanted to know his best advice for success. It was a bold request, but his friend's father agreed and taught Lance something that he has never forgotten, even to this day: "Find what you want to do. Then go find a mentor that is great at what you want to do. Then do as they tell you."

Simple enough, right? Find a mentor, listen to them and take action. Going along with the principle of finding mentors is the Law of Association. Many of us have heard of the Law of Association that states we are the sum of the five people we hang around most.

If you become guilty by association, why not associate with
six, seven or eight-figure earners. — Cedrick Harris

Robert Hollis has created 46 million dollar earners and says the following on finding a mentor: "If you want to learn to dance, martial arts, acting, gymnastics, etc. wouldn't you find a documented instructor and follow their instructions? Find someone who is documented and successful to mirror and match."

If your closest friends are gang members, what sort of Credibility will you have? If your closest friends are all multi-millionaires, what will your Credibility and trust with others be? Do you actually practice the Law of Association? Do you make a conscious effort to limit your associations with negative and toxic people? Do you do whatever is necessary to surround yourself with people that are better than you so that you, too, can grow. The rising tide lifts all ships.

The Law of Association is not to be applied for just making money. This law applies for everything in your life. If you want to become more spiritual, you can't hang around five people who are anti-spiritual. If you want to have a strong marriage, you can't associate with people who are cheating on their spouses. If you want to get in shape, you can't hang around five people who are extremely overweight and don't value being in shape.

No one is perfect and each one of us has flaws, but one of the best ways to become who you want to be is to hang around those who are already who, what, and where you want to be. You need to be honest with yourself. If you brush this idea off as unimportant, then you will never aspire to be around the kind of people you know you should be. You will become what you surround yourself with.

Whether we want to accept that we are practicing the Law of Association or not, it is affecting us every time we choose to hang around people. The people we surround ourselves with rub off on us little by little as we subconsciously learn and become more like our surroundings. Just about everything, including how we talk, act, laugh, and dress, are affected by who we hang around with.

Here's another interesting way to look at the Law of Association. People are energy (or lack thereof). When you associate with dull personalities, you will not dream as big as when you are surrounded by ambitious personalities. Sometimes we are associated with a best friend or a family member whom we may love dearly but they always seem to tear us down. They may not personally attack us, but their lack of ambition and constant negativity bring us down to their level.

For every friend or family member that has negative vibes, you need at least three friends who are extremely positive to make up the difference. It's crazy that one person with negative vibes can have such a profound effect on us. How you dress, think, vote, and everything you do is very closely aligned to those you associate with. Don't ever underestimate the power of the Law of Association. It affects all of us tremendously.

I remember when I made a decision that I wanted to take my life to another level. I believed in the principle of surrounding myself not just with great people but also with great personal development books as well. Instead of just having a few physical mentors, which I had, I also had hundreds of audio mentors. Over the course of about 18 months, I read hundreds of these types of books.

I didn't listen to the radio; instead, I would listen to audio books. I didn't listen to music at the gym; instead I listened to personal development books. I rarely watched TV, in fact, in my first six months in network marketing, as mentioned earlier, I eliminated TV. I substituted that TV time with reading uplifting books. But I didn't just read these books, I studied them. I ended up having hundreds of pages of notes from my readings. I surrounded myself with positive voices on a daily basis. It made me mentally tough.

Those books gave me focus, perspective, discipline, and hope. Read books. Educate yourself. The person you will become will make your current self-esteem seem like that of a kindergartner. And that is an exciting thought!

Your greatness is limited only by the investments
you make in yourself. —Grant Cardone

MASTERING THE LAW OF ASSOCIATION

Imagine knowing and having connections with every important person in your industry that you'll need for the rest of your life. Pretty powerful, right? Well, Troy Dooly has mastered that by practicing the Law of Association.

Troy knows everyone and has become a go-to man as a consultant for many companies in the network marketing industry. Troy's connections are beyond ridiculous, and in a good way! His knowledge is impeccable, but because of his associations, his knowledge isn't just about what he knows, it is what his network knows. Because Troy has so much Credibility within the industry, if you are associated with him, you are associated with just about all of the top industry leaders. His stamp of approval (or lack thereof) can connect or disconnect you with all of the top industry leaders because of the Law of Association.

It isn't easy to avoid negative people with whom you have a strong past connection. Old habits die hard! Old habits scream and crawl their way to the forefront of your mind and actions if you do not consciously put yourself in an environment to squash them. If you do not want to sever that particular relationship, then you must set the guidelines. A compromise will not suffice; you must be blunt and let this particular friend know what you expect. You may not be able to change someone, but you are in control of how you let other people affect you.

The more success someone has had, the more they will typically encourage you to go for your dreams. My experience at the tennis club, when I had no business experience and only a strong vision, was such a powerful learning experience. I was surrounded by others who had been very successful. What I learned is that almost all who have been successful love to give advice and help others be successful.

Think of three people that you know who have been very successful. These could be network marketers, lawyers, your parents, a coach, whoever. Go tell those individuals your goals and dreams. Don't just settle for telling them your small goals. Go all in and tell them your BHAG's: Big Hairy Audacious Goals. The more you let them in on your big dreams, the more they will respect you. Let them know you would love for them to help mentor you and that you will be very coachable. If you do this authentically, without a hidden agenda, I can almost guarantee that you will receive help. How great is that? You will get free help from someone who has been incredibly successful. On that rare occasion where they are not open to mentor you, they might not be the right mentor to begin with. Be persistent, show them you are committed, and if they are still not interested, find someone who's a success and is willing to mentor you.

Not only do you receive a mentor, which I believe is critical for massive success, but you also receive a mentor who will have an incredible circle of influence. They can help introduce you to the right people. You will be amazed at the connections successful people have. Chances are they got those connections from networking consistently as well.

Can you imagine having the opportunity to interview hundreds of the very best network marketers of all time? Can you imagine what you would learn if you were able to interview top leaders on a daily basis? The Networking Times is the premier place to get behind-the-scenes stories trainings from top network marketing icons. Josephine and Chris Gross are the founders of The Networking Times. This was one of the places I was able to study lots of the commonalities of the successful leaders in network marketing. I would highly recommend that you subscribe to it and learn from the legends.

I personally had a goal of being featured in their magazine and in their blogs, and eventually was able to do both. My blog post "The Psychology of the Close" was featured as the #1 blog post for all of 2015 for The Networking Times. There is no way to account for the impact that Credibility brought to my business, but it also had a profound impact in helping to build my Credibility inside the network marketing world. It started with me learning from so many successful mentors and continued with me being able to become one of those featured mentors, which brought a whole new level of Credibility.

> *Friends won't start supporting you until 'strangers'*
> *start celebrating you.* — Unknown

COMMUNICATION CONUNDRUMS

Who knew that five simple words would become so powerful! Has there ever been a more powerful line in all of movie history than "Luke, I am your father"? While there are many lines that are just as recognizable, Darth Vader telling Luke Skywalker that he is his father was not only the ultimate plot twist, but it added to the *Star Wars* legacy that is going to survive and flourish for many generations. Anyone that wasn't living under a rock knew exactly what that scene was about and what movie series it came from.

Our ability to communicate is so ridiculously crucial that even one sentence, like Darth Vader's, can completely set off a plethora of people thinking in a certain way. Effective communication can lead to educated debates, inspiration, guidance, conversations, and especially an increase in building your Credibility!

Communication is often overlooked, but it is what starts and, many times, ends friendships. Wars can begin and end all through communication. Marriage is the most important committed relationship we enter into, and communication, or the lack thereof, is often the reason for either a good marriage or a bad one. Learning to leverage the Power of Communication is a necessary task if you are going to become an expert networker.

THE WORST NETWORKER IN THE WORLD

Demands, broken agreements, and then the cajones to pitch me his business a year later are just a few of the 'incredible' attributes this man possesses. Yes, that last sentence was sarcastic.

Oh, Jim. When will you ever learn?

We will call him Jim because that's his real name. Jim wanted to go work for a company that I owned, so I sent him out to embark on this new venture. He had been asking me for a job for months, and I was so happy because I finally found what I thought to be a great fit for him. Before leaving to start this new job, Jim asked for a signing bonus. I was very upfront with Jim letting him know that was not possible. He agreed and moved across the country to start this new job. So far, so good!

After one week, Jim demanded that I pay him a signing bonus or he would quit. First off, demanding something from someone that offered you an opportunity is never a good thing. Secondly, I made it very clear before he moved that a signing bonus was not possible, and I again told him that wasn't possible. I couldn't get a hold of Jim for the next two days as he went M.I.A. Of course, I was beyond frustrated! I could have easily reacted with my emotions and fired him, but I instead decided to respond cautiously to the situation and evaluate my options. There's a big difference between reacting and responding.

I realized I had a choice. I could just fire him; I could let him quit; or I could pay him the signing bonus. As I ran through those options, I realized there was no way this guy would be a fit for our company. I made it very clear that there would be no signing bonus before he started, and the fact that he is now threatening to quit if he doesn't get his bonus shows me that he's not mentally in the right place. I knew it just wasn't going to work out with us. Rather than lash out at him, which at this point would only make me feel good for a few minutes, I came up with a different option.

I called some local competitors. I was upfront with them on the exact situation. I let them know this guy wasn't a fit for us, but he could be for them. I gave this competitor a caution as my experience wasn't the best but also pointed out Jim's strengths. I then tried calling Jim to let him know I had found a potential better fit for him. The best part is that this new company was willing to give him a bonus if he just simply proved himself for a few weeks. This company was going to give him exactly what he wanted!

Not surprisingly, Jim didn't answer when I called him. So I sent him a text with all the info of a new company in the same industry willing to meet his needs. I thanked him and let him know I was sorry we couldn't meet his needs. I then called the competitors and gave them Jim's phone number. I coached the competitors on how to best handle him. Sure enough, the new company and Jim worked it out, and Jim worked with this new company for two weeks. Jim never once responded to me. He never apologized or thanked me. After two weeks with this new company, he had burnt that bridge with them as well. My competitors were still extremely grateful for the offer.

The story with Jim doesn't end there. Some five months later, Jim sent me a text asking me to check out a "new entrepreneurial venture" he was starting. Really?!?! Some people just don't get it! Not only did Jim lose out on two very high potential jobs, but he lost massive Credibility. It wasn't just because of his worth ethic or entitlement; it was mainly due to his lack of communication. If Jim would have simply communicated with me, I think he could have salvaged a lot of his Credibility and maybe even some of his Likeability.

Here's an example of what Jim could have said without changing his actions and still maintaining much of his Credibility: "Rob, I just wanted to thank you for connecting me to your competitors. I want to apologize for my actions. I am desperate for money and mishandled the situation. I am a hard worker and there is no excuse for the way I dealt with you. If there is anything I can ever do to help you, please let me know how. I hope we can work together again someday in the near future." Those simple words would have completely changed my outlook on Jim. He didn't do it because that's just not who Jim is, which is too bad because I have had several other options I think I could have helped him with.

Always communicate! Admit when you're wrong and be humble. No one's perfect, we all make mistakes. Communication is the key to overcoming mistakes and maintaining credibility. It can be hard and uncomfortable at times but I promise you that communicating will always be better than not. Not communicating will lead to less Credibility, and as a result less Likability. It will often lead to burnt bridges, and we've already discussed that's not what you want. If you continuously have bad communication, then you will become one of the biggest enemies of success: An Avoider.

DON'T BE THE AVOIDER

The more I network, the more I realize how important communication is in building both Likeability and Credibility. Avoiders are so annoying and Jon is no exception. Jon is a great guy and a bad communicator. He was a third party contractor for a company that I owned and had been referred to me from a friend. We created some very basic terms, as a trial to see if he was a fit for us and us for him. He wanted to do business with us, and we needed his services. Now, Jon is one of those people that, when the going gets tough, completely avoids people instead of communicating. We all know a Jon.

After a few weeks of work, Jon asked for a solid contract with every last little detail. To be honest, I wasn't really sure what he wanted specifically, so I put the ball in his court. I asked him to come up with a contract that he felt was fair. After a week's time I hadn't heard from him. This was odd because he was actually doing some great work.

Then, I got a text message that said he was too busy to work for my company. I tried calling Jon several times to no avail. I asked him if he could work for us for just two more weeks to finish off the jobs he had started. I even offered to pay him all of my profits, as I wanted to take care of my clients. Jon wouldn't respond. I ended up calling my friend who had referred him and asked for his help to straighten this out. My friend pleaded with Jon to finish what he had started, but Jon said he was too busy with new jobs from another company and couldn't make the time. Leaving someone in a bind is bad enough, but not communicating with them is like giving them the middle finger.

It doesn't matter that Jon did excellent work for me while he was working. He completely lost all Credibility by being an Avoider. While I know I definitely don't want to do business with him again, there is a larger ripple effect that stems from this. I was very professional and certainly did not deserve to be treated the way I was. Since Jon had no issues doing that to me, I can imagine that is not his first time totally dropping the ball on someone. As such, I won't give him a referral, and I can't ever recommend him to anyone.

It is more than likely that ignoring people, like he did to me, is a regular occurrence for him. That is the biggest issue. If he wanted to part ways, that's ok! However, parting on bad terms hurt him in many more ways than he can imagine. People like Jon don't get it and never find true success.

We may feel that we never do this, and it is easy to look at Jon's story and think to yourself, "Oh, I've never done that before!" However, this same thing happens quite often in network marketing. We might be in the middle of the process of exposing our prospect, and then they just disappear. They seemed interested, they were asking questions, they were engaged, and POOF! It's like they vanish into thin air! They never respond to your messages, they don't call you back, and you know they're ignoring you because they're still posting on Instagram.

Many people would be upset by that scenario, but I actually really enjoy those moments! If that prospect doesn't even have the professionalism to let me know they are no longer interested, then I could only imagine what a disaster they would be if they had chosen to get started. As soon as something bad happened in their business, I am positive they would just disappear off the face of the earth and quit their business. They would also probably blame you for their lack of success, because that's how these people are! We've all dealt with prospects like this, and we've also probably been like this ourselves before. Someone has asked us to do a favor, or maybe they've even asked us for more information about our business, and we just totally blew them off. If we don't like it when people do that to us, then let's work on not being that person as well. It works both ways!

WIFED

Let's pause this book for just a minute and explain how I got wifed! If you are married, you know what it means to get wifed. I sure hope that by reading this book, you don't think that I am a master at everything I am teaching. If you do, then please just call my wife and she will tell you that I still have a ton to work on!

My wife recently called me out. We are always getting together with different groups of people. We recently were with a particular group. I said, "I just don't relate to this group and it takes too much energy to hang around them." Well that was definitely the wrong thing to say!

I should have followed my own advice on multiple ways with this situation. My wife said, "If it has value, you will figure it out. It just takes effort. This group means something to me, so make the effort." If she had a microphone, she would have dropped it and walked away. She may have also nicely said, "you need to follow the advice you are writing in your book.' I just got WIFED, and I deserved it. She was spot on. The next time we hung out with that group, I followed her advice and made a huge effort. It made all of the difference, and I actually enjoyed myself. Also my engagement with this group not only built up my LIKEABILITY with my wife, but it built up my Credibility by listening to my wife.

I may wear the pants in our relationship but my wife decides the color, brand, and size! If the relationship has value, you will find a way to make it work; if you don't, then you're next in line to get WIFED.

THE 3 VERSIONS OF YOU

All human beings have three lives: public, private,
and secret. —Gabriel García Márquez

Every great networker will tell you to become more like the person you want to attract. The only problem is, the person that you may see in public is totally different than how that person acts in private. If you try to change your public self to better emulate another person's public self, the relationship may feel off because who you are in public and who you are in private can be totally different people. I can't think of a better way to describe this concept than by describing the three lives we all live.

I can't think of any topic that will genuinely build your Credibility better than this topic. This is one of the most in-depth concepts that has changed my life. I mentioned that you are who you attract. I love networking because it helps me to become a better person. I believe that the goal is to align our three selves as closely as possible.

Your public self is the one that everyone sees. It is typically most people's best self. Your private self is the one that your friends and family see. They get to see you when you are starving, sick, and just in a bad mood! Your secret self is special; only you know it. What do you do when no one knows? If you could unethically receive $200 from the bank without anyone ever finding out, what would you do? It isn't easy by any means, but your goal should be to match all three lives. Tiger Woods was a perfect example of having a totally different public and secret self. Eventually, it came out. It almost always comes out.

One entire network was destroyed overnight. It happened this way. Years ago, I had a leader whose public self was very well respected. He had a good solid organization that was growing. One day while out of town, this leader, who we will call Jared, decided to check into his hotel with five other team members. As Jared checked in, he looked at this team and said, "Watch this." He then proceeded to lie to the hotel manager and insinuated that he planned to come back to this very hotel with well over 100 people but first wanted to check out the place. The manager gave Jared two free nights to stay, as he hoped this would gain Jared's business.

This was Jared's first lie, but it didn't stop there. In the hotel room, Jared took a needle that he used regularly for steroids to bulk up and put it on the couch. Jared then proceeded to call the hotel manager to complain profusely about a random needle laying around. He said, "Do your maids even clean up the room?!" Of course, the manager apologized and then later gave Jared what he wanted: an upgraded suite for free.

The very next morning, I received a call from a leader who was staying with Jared. This leader explained to me everything that I mentioned above and that there is no way he could trust Jared, which meant there was no way he could follow Jared. He was very distraught because he had made a big financial sacrifice traveling out of state for the event with many from his team. Relationships are about trust. When the trust is gone, it is very difficult to build it back up.

Because of this incident, Jared lost the trust of his entire organization. They saw into his personal life and didn't like who he was. A few months later, no one was making new calls. No one was showing up to events. All business activity came to a complete halt.

This story illustrates the power of matching your different selves as closely as you possibly can. If all of us were judged only on our worst moments, all of us would be guilty. This story about Jared is not to throw him under the bus as he still has incredible potential. It is simply to give you a real-life story that illustrates the power of your different selves.

Leaders are pathfinders. Your organization looks to everything you do. In fact, everyone you know looks to everything you do. As I said before, you are either making deposits of trust or you are taking out withdrawals of trust. Two of the greatest leaders of our time are Gandhi and Mother Teresa. Both of these leaders closely aligned their public, private, and secret selves. They were able to build some of the largest, most loyal networks we have ever seen.

CHAPTER 4

THE CREDIBILITY
CODE

HOW TO BUILD CREDIBILITY THROUGH YOUR APPEARANCE

We all know that looks matter. What most of us don't understand is just how much looks matter and how difficult it is for us to ignore a person's appearance when making a social judgment. —Leonard Mlodinow

Bill Gates can dress as he pleases, but you aren't Bill Gates. You can't afford to not look the part until you are the part. When you are a massively successful individual, your appearance is still important, but it isn't as relevant because you have accumulated both your wealth and Credibility. Until that glorious day comes, you need to do everything you can to create that Credibility. We want that first impression to be strong. We want any extra edge or advantage we can get.

Who do you want to be perceived as? Dress the part. The rule of thumb is to always dress a little nicer than the attire of your audience. If you dress down it can appear very arrogant. There will be times where you can dress up or dress down, but always dress in a style that says SUCCESS. Dress the part, but always be you.

Some make the mistake of over-dressing, while others make the mistake of under-dressing. I myself have made the mistake of under-dressing too many times! It is better to err on the over-dressing side then it is on the under-dressing side. One thing I have noticed is how, at big events, the most successful people in the room stand out because of the way they are dressed. Coincidence? I think not! You want to fit in wherever you are. You want to be the best version of you and look sharp. Looking the part has never hurt anyone, while not looking the part has killed many opportunities.

As a bounty hunter, I have to dress the part. If I came to the door and looked like Carrot Top, you'd laugh. —Duane Chapman

Be You!

How do you make sure you look the part? Always dress to the situation, even if that means dressing like a million bucks! Dress like the person you want to become. Dress like the person you want others to perceive you as. Make sure your suits, shirts, and pants fit well. There is nothing worse than someone wearing clothes that don't fit well. Shoes are also very important. You can wear a decent outfit, but the shoes can turn you from looking homeless to looking like a total, massive success. Appearance is obviously more than just dressing, but remember you are your brand.

Can you imagine Coca Cola putting out an awful marketing advertising campaign or an awful looking can? Now try imagining one of your local awful TV commercials. I know you have them because we all have them. You know those commercials, where you wonder how they came up with such a dumb idea and why they spent money on it. Now imagine Coca Cola doing that for the last five years. It is unfathomable. The main point is that a good product alone isn't enough. Just like you having an incredible skillset isn't enough, your brand is important and constantly in the spotlight, especially because of the advance of social media.

You can't sell a dream looking like
a nightmare — Darryl Drake

People will notice everything, and they will try to drag you down for it. Go get your teeth whitened. Pluck those eyebrows! Trim those nose hairs and get consistent, sharp looking haircuts. Looks are important, and they do make a difference. Even those who claim they could not care less about how they look typically feel better when they are dressed really well and others notice. I am by no means telling anyone to base their self-esteem and confidence on appearance, but I am showing you the reality that appearance matters. Appearance can definitely give you confidence. Don't be vain and worldly and get too caught up in these things. Don't make them your main focus, but do pay attention to your appearance and how you want to represent yourself.

Just imagine a realtor selling you a house dressed in a tank top or a financial advisor selling you life insurance wearing a swimsuit. Dressing the part will give you confidence, and it will also give others confidence that you are the right person. In the book *The Sell*, the author, top New York real estate broker Fredrik Eklund, says this about appearance: "Imagine everyday as a first date. There are so many things we can't control. Appearance is the one thing we can control."

Mike Sims says, "Dress how you want to be addressed." He has his trademark bow ties and top-of-the-line fitted suits and is always dressed like the multi-million dollar earner that he is. He dresses as smooth as he talks, and he stands out! I am always interested in seeing what his next top-of-the-line, stand out suit will look like and that has become part of his brand.

How's your appearance and brand? Do they match up? Would you be attracted to doing business with you if you pulled any of your social media accounts up? As social media outlets have grown, they have had a huge influence on the importance of appearance. We are not only more aware of fashion trends, but with the constant pictures posted on every social media website, we also dress up more often to look good for our shared pictures. I know that may sound funny to a few, but most of you know that this is absolutely true! You are your brand. Wear it well.

Want to know one of the easiest ways to look (and feel) like a million bucks? Get in shape! When you are in shape, you are healthier. That should in itself be enough reason to be in shape, but it also shows you are a disciplined person. You can set goals, work hard, and have success. When you are capable of doing that in one aspect of your life, it usually means you will be able to in other areas as well.

When you are in shape you are also more attractive. I know that sounds superficial, but again let's be honest with each other. Would you network and recruit better at an optimal body fat percentage or at 600 lbs.? I know that's an extreme example, but I hope it gets the point across. Again, don't take this the wrong way; I know a lot of successful networkers who are overweight. We also all know several examples of overweight celebrities that have found ways to use their weight as part of their persona. Being overweight doesn't make or break someone, but I think everyone can agree being in great shape can only help you in all aspects of life, networking included.

There is a huge difference between being fit versus fat, literally! Being fit will make you feel better about yourself, give you more energy, lead to a longer and better quality life, and give you more opportunities for happiness. As mentioned earlier in this book, happiness is a large piece of building your Likeability, and it's really hard to be credible if someone doesn't initially like you.

Getting in shape is a scary commitment for a lot of people, but it doesn't have to be. Instead of thinking about how much you have to work out or how you have to eat healthier, take it day by day, choice by choice. Choose the healthier option when eating a meal over the unhealthier one. Decide to get up half an hour earlier so you can schedule in the time to work out, even if it's just a few exercises from home. Start small and work your way up.

I have been extremely consistent with going to the gym ever since I was 16 years old. I am not extremely buff or anything, but I am in great shape. As someone who grew up playing tennis, I value being healthy more than packing on muscle. Going to the gym consistently since 2008 without missing a week has helped me maintain a healthy lifestyle. It makes it easier to choose healthier food choices. I have more energy, I feel better about myself, and I have been able to take that same discipline and apply it to my business. The only workouts I ever regret are the ones I don't do! It has gotten to the point that it is more painful to miss the gym than it is to go to the gym. I am always in a better mood on the days that I go to the gym and get a good workout in.

> *Man surprised me most about humanity. Because he sacrifices his health in order to make money. Then he sacrifices money to recuperate his health. And then he is so anxious about the future that he does not enjoy the present; the result being that he does not live in the present or the future; he lives as if he is never going to die, and then dies having never really lived.* — Dalai Lama

Modern Leadership

> *I'm going to do it with or without but I would rather do it with you.* — Ray Higdon

Modern day leadership more than ever involves the Law of the Buy-In. There are many different aspects to the Law of the Buy In. Go back to what I have already taught you: people want to feel important. That is a very basic, yet profound, aspect to understand when you are making friends and networking. A critical part to making teammates feel important is to make them feel a part of what is being created. Involving others the right way, having them buy in, will increase your Credibility.

Many times I have seen employees leave jobs with good pay to go to new jobs with lesser pay simply because they didn't feel like they were able to contribute at their old job. They didn't feel important. They didn't feel valued. If the boss simply made those employees feel like they were part of decisions, they would have felt important and the leader's Credibility would have been greatly increased. Always get the buy-in whenever you can. People will become loyal to ventures they help create. They will buy in to what they help create.

The other aspect to the Law of the Buy-In is getting the leaders to 'buy-off.'

If you are an employee trying to get your boss to approve your idea, you should find a way to get your boss's opinion and feedback throughout the process. If you are creating a new system for your network marketing team, go get some of the other leaders to help create the system. Anyone who helps you create something will be more loyal to what was created. If you want to ever get leaders to say yes then get their advice, get them to feel like their ideas are implemented, and ultimately get their buy-in.

John Maxwell gives a different take on being a leader and getting others to buy into you:

> *The Law of Buy-In—People buy into the leader, then the vision. The leader finds the dream and then the people. The people find the leader and then the dream. That's how the Law of Buy-In works. People don't at first follow worthy causes. They follow worthy leaders who promote worthy causes they can believe in. People buy into the leader first, then the leader's vision. As a leader, having a great vision and a worthy cause is not enough to get people to follow you. You have to become a better leader; you must get your people to buy into you. That is the price you have to pay if you want your vision to have a chance of becoming reality. You cannot ignore the Law of Buy-In and remain successful as a leader.*

People commit to what they create. Let people help you create something and feel that it was their idea.

Even the greatest and most powerful CEOs in the world can't help but feel like a kid on Christmas if you do this one thing correctly. One of the companies I consulted for asked me and a few others to create a new brand. The CEO couldn't even remember my name for the first couple months. I knew we needed to get his buy-in to make this project work.

I made it a point to meet with him and, rather than tell him how much I knew, I simply applied the Benjamin Franklin factor and asked him for advice. Remember, Franklin teaches you to ask for advice from your enemies or those who don't like you, but the Ben Franklin Factor still applies to anyone. People tend to like people who ask them for a favor or advice. After I had spent months creating a name, culture, systems, and price points for products, all while finding other leaders to buy into this new initiative, the CEO finally knew my name.

I asked him to help us create this new initiative and also asked if I could meet on a regular basis to make sure that this project was on the right course. After paying the CEO respect, asking for his advice on what had been created and for help for all future decisions, I had his buy-in. I knew it didn't matter if we created the greatest program in the world if we didn't have the buy-in from the CEO.

A year later, the CEO felt like this was his project. He felt like he had created this new initiative. In reality, he didn't create anything, but he supported everything that was created. Networking, business, and friendships are about creating the best possible outcome. In order to do so, you need to follow the law of the buy-in and you can't worry about who gets the credit. You can make a lot of money if you don't get easily offended and focus instead on giving others credit.

There is no limit to the amount of good you can do if you
don't care who gets the credit — Ronald Reagan

Not only do I have experience of getting others to buy in, but I have bought-in-to someone myself! The very first time I met Jordan Adler, the author of *Beach Money*, I was shocked at the questions he asked me. He is very well-known and respected in the network marketing world. I hadn't been introduced with any sort of background, so Jordan had no idea if I was wildly successful or a brand-new network marketing distributor. I told him I enjoyed his book. He immediately started asking me for advice on which title I liked best for the new book that he was writing. I walked away feeling important, thinking, "Wow, what a great guy Jordan is, asking me for advice when he has no idea my background." He immediately gained more Credibility in my eyes and won me over as a fan.

It didn't take much, but Jordan Adler had his Credibility shoot up through the roof by asking me just a few simple questions and getting me to buy-in. By feeling more involved with the process, I bought-in to what Jordan is all about, and his Likeability soared through the roof. Anytime you can raise your Likeability significantly in a single transaction, you are going to raise your Credibility as well. The same can be said for increasing your Credibility. It will increase your Likeability. Both will help raise the other.

HIGH LIKEABILITY BUILDS HIGH CREDIBILITY

What can you do to build your Credibility? There are five key factors to focus on when building your Credibility. All things being equal, your likeability will be the key to winning the tiebreaker. One of the greatest things about building up your Likeability is that it helps to build Credibility. People like people that exercise these Rules.

Let's say you meet two people that are both very smart on the same topic. As you talk to them, one of them smiles at you and the other one doesn't at all. Which one will you think is more credible? Probably the person that smiled at you, even though a smile has nothing to do with the Credibility of the content he is telling you. Instinctively, you are more trusting of the person that smiled at you because of that built Credibility.

Building your own Credibility comes through both your actions and your ability to become a great communicator. Communicating properly builds trust, which builds Credibility. When it comes to building your Credibility, there are five laws that come into play.

1. THE FIRST LAW IS TIME

We all seemingly don't have enough of it. Everyone is always busy, or in a rush. Because of this, it is important that we not only value our time but the time of the person we are communicating with. It can be very easy to point fingers and accuse certain people of having no respect for other's time, but let's not play the blame game. I know you hate it when someone wastes your time over and over again, so have enough respect for the person you are networking with to limit your time with them and not waste it.

Being late to meet someone shows a lack of respect for their time. Be prompt for all of your appointments, business or social. If you are running late, show respect and courtesy by letting them know. Something as simple as this boosts your Credibility and Likeability because you are showing respect for the other person.

Time management on your part will help you respect other people's time. Always plan on being ten minutes early, in case something goes wrong. In order to help you be ten minutes early, always plan on each task taking longer than expected. Plan for the worst, but hope for the best. If I have a meeting at 1 p.m. that is supposed to last for an hour, but I have no control over it, I will leave myself a buffer of time in between to ensure I am on time, or I will let my 1 p.m. appointment know the exact time I have to leave.

Time management is actually one of my strengths. The simple answer is to plan ahead well, give yourself a buffer, and realize many things take a lot longer than expected. Don't always assume best-case scenarios for; instead, always assume the worst-case scenario. If you show up early, I am sure there are always calls that you can catch up on.

2. THE SECOND LAW IS SUCCESS

Or more specifically, your own success. Learn how to tell your story properly, just like we went over earlier in the book and will touch up on again. People love success stories! With all the negativity reported by the media nowadays, a feel-good story or celebrating someone's success is a big deal! Whether you've had great successes, or a series of small successes, leverage that! People won't give you the time of day if you can't prove your Credibility. This does not mean you go brag to everyone about your accomplishments; rather, find common ground where you can share a success story about yourself that will prove your Credibility and open the door to further conversation.

3. THE THIRD LAW IS LEVERAGING OTHER PEOPLE'S SUCCESS

Learn how to borrow other people's stories. This becomes especially important when you are proving yourself as a mentor that has helped others achieve success. The law of association is very powerful. If someone credible is either associated or working with you, that lends you Credibility. People care about all your accolades and your greatness but most people think, "What's in it for me?" You need to show people your Credibility and open the door for more communication by showing people that you've created success for Person X, Person Y, and Person Z, and you can do the same thing for them. When you are able to show people your proven track record of success, most will want to listen.

One of the greatest lessons a leader can learn is that he or she doesn't need to know all the answers—he or she just needs to know how to pull the answers out of the best people.
—CEO and Founder of the Og Mandino Group, Dave Blanchard

4. THE FOURTH LAW IS COMMITMENT

Commitment is about sticking with your goal through the tough times. It's about not letting anything stand in the way between you and your success. Commitment is also about committing to your team. It's about investing in your people and leading with servant-leadership. The old school "boss" mentality is long gone. People don't like bosses anymore; instead, they like leaders. Bosses demand too much and give too little. Many bosses are considered takers while leaders are givers. Commit to being a leader for both yourself and for your team, and never let there be any doubt in your team's mind about your intentions; this way your belief levels, and those of your entire team, will be elevated. It's harder to quit on someone when you know they won't quit on you.

5. THE FIFTH AND FINAL LAW IS HONESTY

I don't care how amazing you are to someone and how much they look up to you. The first time you lie to them, things will never be the same. Everything you say will be taken with a grain of salt because they know you could be lying. If you've lied once, what's to stop you from doing it again? Honesty is always the best policy, and it is pivotal to your brand and Credibility. Even though it may be tough sometimes to tell the truth, it's a lot harder to have to own up to your lies down the road. Would you rather be known as the person that has lied their way to the top or the one who kept their integrity all the way through?

You know those people that are so likeable that you almost want to punch them? Bob Snyder has been in the direct sales industry for over 20 years. He currently owns a non-MLM direct sales company. The first time I met Bob was at a networking event. He was so likeable with his smile, positive attitude, and charm. As I got to know Bob I wanted to learn more about some of his investments, so I did what I always do: I went around asking other trusted friends if they knew Bob and what their thoughts were of him.

Every single person, without question, told me that Bob was one of the most trusted people they knew. The responses weren't simply, "Sure, Bob is a nice guy." Instead, person after person repeatedly had a strong stance that Bob could be trusted. His authenticity was real, and he had grown a reputation that he was not only likeable, but he could be well trusted.

Above all, success in business requires two things:
a winning competitive strategy,
and superb organizational execution.
Distrust is the enemy of both.
I submit that while high trust won't necessarily
rescue a poor strategy, low trust will almost always
derail a good one. —Stephen M.R. Covey

CHAPTER 5

THE LAW OF
RECALLABILITY

LAW #3

*My mama always said, 'Life was like a box of chocolates.
You never know what you're gonna get.'*

This town ain't big enough for the two of us.

Houston we have a problem.

*Are you crying? Are you crying?! There's no crying!
There's no crying in baseball!*

Can you guess which movies these quotes come from? If you are from my generation, or earlier, these quotes are obvious! They are all quotes from famous movies starring Tom Hanks. Hanks is one the of the top ten highest grossing actors of all-time. He is extremely likeable as a movie character and has created as much Credibility as anyone in the acting world. He has become so recognizable due to his Likeability and Credibility that his movie scenes are very recallable. Whether it is *Forrest Gump, Saving Private Ryan,* Woody from *Toy Story,* or *The DaVinci Code,* you can recall famous Tom Hanks movie scenes.

So, what exactly is Recallability? First off, it's not a word I just made up. Recallability is the ability to have an awareness of something or someone. If you have a high Recallability, you come to mind often. If you have a low Recallability, then no one thinks to network with you. Many times those with low Recallability have high Credibility but are never thought of. You can be likeable and build up tons of Credibility, but if no one can recall you when you would have been the perfect fit for the job, then there's no way you will be profitable! This is a perfect place for me to remind you to go join my Facebook group page, The Game of

Networking. Not only does it help my recallability but it can help yours. This is a great place for you to post valuable content and become more recallable.

There were no storm clouds in the sky or raindrops falling when Noah built his ark. More than likely, the sun was shining and the birds were singing, but, Noah knew better. He was busy chopping down forests, turning them into planks, hammering them together, and building an ark. The days and weeks went by. The months passed and then the floods came and the rest is history. Because Noah prepared himself, he was ready and did not get overtaken by the flood waters.

It takes time to network. The most important time to network is when you don't need anything. Build up your value by building up others with good intentions. If you do, you will build a reservoir that you can use when needed; if you don't, that reservoir will be empty when you need it most. Real relationships aren't convenient. They take time and work. Don't wait until it is too late.

If you want to build a million dollar check you have to
build million dollar relationships. — Clif Braun

You don't go to a garden that hasn't been attended to for months and say, "Why don't I have any tomatoes?!" Any chance of you having beautiful, ripe tomatoes was squandered months before when you made the decision that your tomato garden was not important enough for you to tend to. That decision you made months ago was reinforced every single time you thought about tending to your garden but decided something else was more important. Then, when you really wanted your tomatoes, surprise! There aren't any. By failing to plan, you planned to fail.

Your future will become what you make of it.
If you choose to plan nothing, then nothing is what you'll receive.
However, if you choose success and plan for it...
success is what you'll receive. — Mel Atwood

So much more time needs to be spent on cultivating relationships, building connections, and creating the root system for your network. If you try to pull the product without even letting the roots establish, you will kill off any progress that may have been made. Feed the roots and let the roots grow deep before going in for the kill!

It is worth so much more to help someone when you get nothing out of it at that moment. Think of those moments as your deposits into your emergency savings account. I promise that when you do need something, the favor you receive will be reciprocated in a huge way and well worth all those pesky deposits.

So when I am asked "When is the best time to network?" there really is no best time because you should always be networking! It is called netWORKing for a reason. It takes time and work. Anything worthwhile takes time and work, and great relationships are no exception.

Lisa Grossman is one of those people who is known as one of the most brilliant trainers in all of network marketing. Even more than that, she is always striving to strengthen relationships. It isn't by coincidence that she is one of the most influential leaders in the entire industry. She has NETWORKed. In the first conversation I had with her, she gave me advice for an hour without asking for anything in return. She texted me a week later asking if there was anything she could do to help me and my team. I'm not even in the same company as Lisa, and she still went out of her way to check up on me! Isn't that incredible? She still continues to do this on a regular basis.

Lisa understands the principle of working your network and providing value for others. She is building her ark before it ever rains. If Lisa ever had to start over in network marketing (which she won't have to, but stick with me here), I know she will have no problem rising to the top ranks again because she is no fluke. She has tended to her tomatoes and built her ark so nothing will stand in her way. She has spent countless hours with my team and the teams of other top leaders without any financial gain. She is a master NETWORKer and is easily recallable as one of the top leaders in all of network marketing.

WHEN GETTING NO IS GOLD

Follow me on this. The best invite can be getting a ton of 'no's. That sounds funny and doesn't make sense but let me explain. This technique is gold for Recallability! No, I am not talking about inviting someone to join your network marketing business. I am talking about something completely different.

Let me give you an example. I was given a tee time for four to go golfing last summer. I had three spots to fill for free golf. I filled those spots, but in order to do so, I invited 12 people to go knowing I could only get three to say yes. The tee time was right during the middle of a normal workday so I knew ahead of time most wouldn't be able to go. Even though I knew most couldn't play, I knew the gesture would still go a long way. Of course, I hoped all could go but realistically I knew that wasn't feasible.

Now, think about what I just did. I had three people that I was able to go have fun and connect with, but I also had nine people that felt pretty important that they were invited. I got a ton of goodwill out of simply inviting and being thoughtful of others. Sure, I knew some would say no, but that didn't stop me from inviting them. I can all but guarantee you that each one of those 12 people will have me on the short list the next time they go golfing or the next time they do something fun like that. Even if I had not been given a free tee time for four, I could have applied the same principle just by scheduling a tee time and inviting others.

Be inclusive, and don't stop inviting. Sometimes, my wife and I love just going to the movies with no one else. Other times, we will plan to go with a small group, or, on special occasions, we will go to the movies with a large group. Say you only have room for ten couples. If you are at seven couples, don't stop inviting. Keep inviting until you get to ten! Those who were invited but don't end up coming will feel very important just by the mere fact they were included.

You don't have to have something free to offer others in order for this to work. If you are inclusive and invite others to feel a part of your life, people will feel important and well connected to you. Using this technique the right way is one of the most powerful ways to follow the Law of Recallability.

Please don't misuse this principle. Your intentions are important. My intentions aren't to purposely get told no; I don't hope to get a no. I genuinely love people, and I love the camaraderie of being with others. I always hope for a yes rather than a no. My main point is for you to understand the principle of being inclusive, making others feel important, and how getting a no on your invite can still be a great thing. It is also important to understand the value in no because many fear getting told it, especially in a social setting. It isn't as great as a yes, but there is still is great value.

I have known Greg Merrill since the 8th grade. I lost track of him for several years after high school, but then we ended up being neighbors. Greg is a successful financial advisor who distinguishes himself by networking. I have been invited by him to countless movies, golf outings, ski days, lunches, and many other fun social gatherings. Greg always wants someone to say yes to his invites, but when someone says no, he doesn't freak out. He continually invites others applying the principles taught above. By frequently connecting with so many and by constantly inviting others to many different functions, he has made others feel included. He has turned the connection into the relationship. He has become The Host and made others feel important.

The Host Gets the Most

Leonardo DiCaprio is one of the best actors I know, and he did an excellent job in *The Great Gatsby*. Leo plays Jay Gatsby, an extremely rich and even more mysterious businessman that lives in West Egg, New York, during the Roaring 20s. No one has really met Jay Gatsby (at least at the start of the movie), but everyone knows of him and speaks very highly of him for one reason: he throws the most incredible parties!

Every single weekend, rich and poor, old and young, Wall Street brokers and street sweepers would all meet up at Gatsby's huge mansion for the most amazing parties, complete with magicians, acrobats, singers, dancers, live music, and lots of booze! These lavish parties were a great way for people to come together and network.

Furthermore, even though no one had actually met Gatsby, everyone liked him because he was the Host. Now, I am not telling you to throw wild parties like Jay Gatsby, but becoming the Host will help put your networking on steroids! It's great to be liked. It's even better to be needed. The Host always receives the most appreciation because people are naturally attracted to the leader. This may not be your personality; it may feel uncomfortable, but this is where you must and will shine. This is where you can create some massive value.

You may have read through the Likeability and Credibility sections and found some action points that you can easily apply starting today, like smiling more or never showing up late to events. Putting the Law of Recallability into practice by becoming the Host will be the most labor intensive but also arguably the most rewarding. The Host becomes the go-to person, and any time you can put yourself in a position to hold that kind of power, you should do it!

A Toast to the Host

You can become the host in several different ways. As you can see, many of them start off very small and simple, and it can turn into an incredible experience that leaves a lasting impact on your crowd.
- Dinners at your house
- Invite people to watch sporting events at your house
- Group lunches
- Golf, skiing, or whatever hobby you may enjoy
- Anything fun you have planned, invite some friends

- Christmas/Hanukkah get together
- Halloween get together
- Summer BBQ's
- Visit your neighbors. Knock on their doors. Say hello.
- Go to church
- Get on an H.O.A. board
- Find service groups
- Find networking groups
- Develop a new talent
- Go workout at the gym with a class
- Join a book club

You can start small and have a dinner at your house. Doesn't have to be fancy, just casually having some friends over and getting some good food prepared will do the trick. I would also recommend not inviting all new people. Invite a few new people, but also invite others that you feel comfortable with. This will make the environment much more relaxed and fun. If there is a particular sporting event or even TV show that you like, invite people over to watch with you. If you want to break the ice and really get to know people, play games.

YES, I SAID GAMES.

Before you laugh and blow off this idea, hear me out. Adults like to have fun, and there are plenty of fun games. Playing games and having fun can create a great connection. Who do you think would stand out more: a host that held a dinner where everyone was trying to be really proper and uptight so as to not stand out, or a host that held a dinner and also played games so everyone was relaxed and had a better time? I think you know the answer.

Yes, sometimes just having fun conversations is a good way to start. Or try putting together a gathering that is of interest to your new contact. If you follow these principles and put on your own events, people will have an incredible amount of respect for you. Even more importantly, you will be recalled by those people as they tell stories and share memories of that great time and experience they had with you. You create recallability because you have now injected yourself into these memories and stories that will be shared with others that weren't even there.

If you are looking for network marketing specific events, try to go to the annual GoPro convention, an ANMP (Association of Network Marketing Professionals put on by Garrett and Sylvia McGrath along with several other industry leaders) event, a network marketing cruise, or any and every network marketing event you can. There are many different non-company affiliated network marketing events. Use them to get to know other professionals and your Credibility will go up by the Law of Association. More importantly, you will be able to learn from these professionals.

Eventually, you will make friends with other networkers, and your network will increase dramatically. You will be amazed at how one person can open up an entire new network to you, and the larger your network, the more value you can provide to people, and the more recallable you become. As always, do everything with the right intention! Look to provide value to people. Look to be a good friend always striving to give. Focus more on giving and having the right intentions. If your intent is in the right place, the reward will naturally come.

BIGGER SCALE EVENTS

Marketing is a contest for people's attention. — Seth Godin

Once you become a great networker and you've got the above activities down pat, it's time for you to move on to the bigger events. I know because I've done a number of them. They are always worth it. They could be called Recallability on Steroids!

Colten Shea understands the principle of hosting an event and the social benefits that come along with it. Colten is a young ambitious top industry leader in network marketing. He learned years ago, even before network marketing, that people are attracted to the host. A few years after high school, Colten built up his social influence by simply creating different events. He would throw parties and other fun events at his house, and as the events grew, so did his social influence. Colten became "the guy" to be around because he was the host. The host gets the most!

Social proof is the validation that others like you and want to be associated with you. It almost makes you a low level celebrity in a weird way. Colten understood this principle and started to focus hard on creating great inspirational content, as well as outstanding lifestyle branding, on his social media. He adds everyone to his social media right when he meets them. Once they see his posts, and the number of followers and likes he gets, that becomes his social proof.

Becoming the host and understanding social proof isn't an overnight project. It would be a more advanced strategy for the overachievers. If you aren't running an event, a good tip when supporting an event would be to show up early or stay late. Do this so that you can help out. Helping out the hosts will go a long way! You will stand out and get a chance to better know the host.

Someone that has taken his social proof to the next level is Eric Worre. Eric is the most influential leader in all of network marketing. Everything he touches turns to gold and everything he says comes out just right. How did he become the most influential? He is the #1 host. Remember, the host gets the most!

Years ago, Eric started Network Marketing Pro. His mission is to help network marketers stop being posers and amateurs and to help them make the decision to go pro. His best-selling book, *Go Pro: Seven Steps to Becoming a Network Marketing Professional*, really catapulted him into the spotlight as the premier trainer in the network marketing industry. Every year, he hosts a Go Pro Recruiting Mastery that brings in 20,000+ distributors (not counting those that watch on-line) from all different companies all over the world. The non-company specific training is taught by leaders from across the world, male and female, young and old. Just about every great leader wants to speak at the Go Pro Recruiting Mastery and get their whole team there as well.

The coolest part about hosting big events is that you do not have to make the event network marketing specific. Realtors, brokers, actors and actresses, waiters, computer tech people, construction workers, you name it can also host large events, just like one of the top realtors in all of Utah, Jimmy Rex.

Jimmy Rex is a master at networking through big events. He hosts incredible events just like Jay Gatsby did but without the booze and gambling. He started out with small events and slowly grew them, and now his events are some of the largest in all of Utah. He has a yearly fireworks show where over 5,000 people attend. He consistently rents out movie theatres, giving out free tickets to clients and friends. I attended six of his free movies before I finally used him as a realtor. He has raised over $200,000 to fight sex trafficking. Not once did he ever pitch doing business with me at the movie theater, firework show, or any event that Jimmy threw. Jimmy simply created a fun environment and brought people together.

As I picked Jimmy's brain, he told me he tried to host any type of function he could to get to know new people. He didn't pitch them on business. He just became their friend and always offered to help them in any way he could. As he made more friends with different groups, he was invited to more functions and then he would make those people part of his network. It is a never ending growth cycle for Jimmy, and he understands the host gets the most. Jimmy Rex is likeable and credible but where he stands out even more than anyone else is that he really gets the law of Recallability, and it has made him millions of dollars.

This may all sound overwhelming to you, and it is for most people. This isn't something you have to do. This would be a technique for the overachievers! If anything, you can apply this principle on a smaller scale to help you network. As I mentioned just a few paragraphs earlier, start with group dinners or lunches. Start with planning a movie with other friends and help coordinate. There are so many small ideas that you can implement to start the process. As you do this, you will start to feel more comfortable and your confidence will grow.

Sometimes you will have to use your resources or get creative. I am fortunate that my grandma owns a cabin that I can use to have bigger functions. Twice a year, my wife and I invite lots of couples to the cabin. We always create fun games and coordinate everyone bringing food. In settings like these, it is harder to get to know people, but there is a lot of energy and it is fun connecting with so many people.

When you organize an event, you will be invited to many other people's functions. It is the law of reciprocation. What we give, we receive. This is just a natural process of providing value for others. I know state this often but it is always important to understand the right intentions behind everything you do. You don't host because you expect others to then invite you to everything they do. Some will and some won't, but if you authentically provide value for others you will receive more value back than if you had not provided anything at all. Even more importantly, you feel good about doing it.

Years ago, my wife and I were invited, by Jarom Dastrup, to go to Lake Powell with about 13 couples. I only knew two of the couples going on the trip; however, we are always up for making new friends and we're always looking to have a good time, so we decided to go. We weren't sure what to expect, as many of the others were really good friends already. It is always a little uncomfortable going with a large group of new people who you don't know, but by the end of the trip, my wife and I had made many lifelong connections. To this day, I still frequently go to lunch or get together with many of the friends my wife and I met at Lake Powell.

The Law of Reciprocation was in full effect as years later I was able to help Jarom land a very big job. He was going through a transition in his career. As he is a master networker, he started by calling many from his network to see if they had any connections that were a fit for his personality and skillset. Jarom had multiple offers for high-level jobs from several different industries. He had great options because of his skillset, but those options would not have been available if he had not put the work in to maintain a good network. He had made a tremendous amount of deposits into his emergency networking account, so when it was time for him to receive help finding a new job, he was able to do so very quickly.

Had Jarom not invited me to Lake Powell, I highly doubt that he would have called me to help connect him with a new venture. Since Jarom and I had created a stronger friendship through Lake Powell, he felt 100 percent confident in asking me for help. He is currently in a very prominent role in a $100+ million networking company and I couldn't be happier that I was able to help a good friend.

In 2012, I planned an 80's style dodgeball tournament, for my wife's birthday. I know, it is totally random, but it was a lot of fun! You may not want to be active in your events, and that is ok. My goal is to give you examples of what I have done to help get your creative juices flowing!

On a different year, we went to the famous Pirate's Cove, one of the greatest places on earth, hands down. Go YouTube Pirate's Cove and you will see for yourself, but the video doesn't do it justice.

Pirate's Cove is owned by a very successful individual. It is pirate themed with three pools and 21 master suites. I was able to rent out this place for three different groups in one week. Over 240 people attended with each family pitching in their share of the total cost. This was obviously a large scale event and was a ton of work, but I can tell you it was one of the most rewarding networking experiences I have ever had. I am not talking about results, as those are hard to quantify. I am speaking specifically about how great it felt to provide a fun experience for so many.

Bottom line is that you need to become the organizer. Being the host signifies leadership, and people are attracted to leadership. As John Maxwell says, "Leadership is influence. Nothing more. Nothing less." The organizer typically becomes the leader. When you are providing value for others, they naturally want to find a way to reciprocate that value. People will naturally want to be around you more. Becoming recallable will be simple if people are making efforts to be around you and interact with you, but that won't happen unless you first are that way to them. It isn't what you know or who you know, but who knows you!

Over four million online views annually from 150 plus different countries is enough to get anyone's attention. Ever heard of Ted Nuyten? If not, have you ever heard of "Business for Home?" Ted was once a distributor in the network marketing industry. He decided that he wanted to create more validity to the industry, so he created a website sharing the incomes of other distributors. He had no idea at the time but he quickly found a huge niche and Business for Home was born. It is the top online news and recognition site available by a long shot. Ted makes a ton of money, and deservedly so. He is the top online host and, as we learned, the host gets the most. Even as you learn how to become the host you will still need to master the techniques I teach in my free eBook on how to taproot. Don't forget to download your free eBook at www.robsperry.com/blueprint/.

Starting Young

Learning how to host and network properly starts at a young age. You should teach your kids to network, whether you are a parent now or a future parent. Teaching your kids to network will be one the most valuable skills you can ever teach them. Becoming the host also applies to your kids as well. Have your kids host small get-togethers or parties. Remember, people migrate towards the host. There are several ideas you can implement with your kids that are simple, depending on your kids' ages. You can find a local pool during the summer or simply have a movie night. Encourage your kids to compliment others and to invite over new friends. Remember, networking not only increases success, but it is one of the keys to happiness

The Law of 250

Joe Girard is listed in the *Guinness Book of World Records* as "The Best Salesman in the World" because of a few strategies he implements better than anyone else. It seems like a difficult thing to get a concrete title for, but there are stats to back that up. Over the course of his 14-year car salesman career, he has sold over 13,000 vehicles. That's an average of more than three per day! On his best day, he ended up selling 18 cars. By himself, he has sold more cars than 95% of all of the dealers in North America. How does one person become so exceptionally good at sales?

The Law of 250, which Girard came up with himself, states that the average person has about 250 people in their lives that would show up to their funeral or wedding. Some have more and some have less, but the average is about 250. To Joe, this meant that for every bad pitch he did when trying to sell a car, he lost a potential 250 referrals. However, for every good pitch he did that ended up with a car being sold, he gained a potential 250 referrals.

Girard would keep records of every single customer who bought from him. He would follow up with them and take notes on not just how they liked their car but also about their personal lives. He would write down all of their kid's names and what sports they played so he could develop a personal relationship with them and show that he cares about his customers for more than just their business. Last but not least, he always asked for referrals. Because of the great relationships he built, he didn't come off as someone who was "salesy" when asking for referrals. In fact, his customers were more than happy to refer their friends to Girard, and almost every single one of Girard's 13,000+ sales over 14 years were from referrals.

Every time one of Girard's past customers knew someone was in the market looking for a car, that customer would automatically think of Girard and have no problem recommending him, because he had high recallability. This would not have been possible if Girard did not do the little, mundane tasks like keeping records of all his customers or following up about his customer's personal lives. How would your income grow if you had over 13,000 referrals in your career? Talk about putting the Law of Recallability to work!

It always pays to go the extra mile for your customer to build a relationship. So many people try to shove their own wants and needs down the throats of their prospects, and the prospects hate that! People like to feel loved and respected, and that is what good relationships are built upon. Take the extra time to care about what your prospects care about, and watch how fast your network grows.

Girard was the top car salesman and he wasn't salesy. If you have a fear of sales, get over it! We all sell in just about everything we do in life! I sold myself to my wife to get married. My kids sell me on getting fruit snacks every day. You sell yourself on getting a job or getting a promotion. There is nothing wrong or scary about selling. What's scary is taking advantage of someone for your own gain. The greats aren't takers. The greats find a need and fill it by good solid communication.

The reason why most people struggle is that they never understand the difference between selling and marketing. If you want to be successful in your business then you have to learn how to STOP selling and START marketing. — Bob Heilig

WHAT NOT TO DO: THE RECALLABILITY HAS BEENS

The "Has Beens" are those that made a good amount of money years ago. Some of them got lucky and everything went their way, and some of them truly built their organization. Either way, they ride on their past Credibility and stop networking. They lose influence with their current group because they are not engaged in the business. They also stop staying in touch with most people and lose influence of their network. As soon as a leader leaves their group or the company struggles, their income goes down. Once their income goes down, many try to re-engage to build their business back up.

I have referred often to the mentality that rich people think long term while poor people think short term. Their nearsightedness costs them dearly. Networking is the perfect example of building your ark before it rains. Remember, the best time to network is when you don't need anything. Always be making deposits of goodwill so that when you need to take withdrawals, you have enough goodwill saved up!

Once you become a leader, don't be arrogant and forget how you got there. Don't be that "has been" leader who does too little, too late. It doesn't work. You can't skip the basic success principles and still expect success because "once upon a time" you had success. You are never above those success principles. Success is earned each and every time. Success is like rent. You must keep paying rent or you will fail.

I am currently in the trenches which means that I am working on a daily basis with my organization. I am leading by example from the front with my actions and not just my words. There will be a time in my life when I am no longer in the trenches. When that time comes, I do not plan on completely checking out. I understand the value of relationships and would never do that.

I do plan on taking summers off. I plan on taking Thanksgiving to New Year's off. I plan to work less but be more efficient with my time. I plan on creating trips for my new leaders in my organization. I want to thank them and help provide mentorship to them. I want to also continue to always strengthen the relationships with my strongest leaders. This business isn't just about you, for you are nothing without your team.

Brian Carruthers is the opposite of a "Has Been." Despite being in the industry since 1994 and having over 400,000 people in his organization, Brian is still in the trenches. He is always making new contacts, leading by example and providing value for his team. At the time of the writing of this book, he is still recruiting new people every day as if he's in his first month in his business. He still takes his job as a sponsor seriously, locking arms with each recruit to do their presentations for them—staying in "Phase One." I have never seen him unplug. (Brian also provides live training videos and industry-wide webinars to help everyone.) He still enjoys life with his family and takes regular vacations as you would expect, but he stays consistent. I would be shocked if he ever becomes a "Has Been" because he is always engaged in helping his teams succeed.

GHOSTING 101

There was a particular company that offered me a very good financial package to consult for them. I connected very well with the top executives of this company and thought they were a great fit for me personality wise, as well as for business. For whatever reason, I decided that my passions weren't aligned with the company's vision, so I turned down their offer. They were shocked. I immediately sent them thank you texts, and a week later, I sent a thank you email. I never heard back, so I figured they just got busy.

Two months went by and I sent another email seeing if they filled the position they offered me. I let them know that if they hadn't, I would love to help connect them with some real sharp, dynamic people who could get the job done. Nothing. Zilch. Nada. I still never heard anything back.

Much time has passed since then, and to this day I still haven't heard a word from this company. I really did connect with them. I still think they are smart and a great group of individuals on both a personal and business level. They are also awful networkers. They don't get it! Not only could they have cultivated a relationship with me that could have led to us working together someday, they also could have tapped into my entire network. I know I could have helped them fill their position. All they needed to do was stay in contact (Recallability) and not turn into ghosts. When I say stay in contact, I really mean just a few times a year. It's not that hard to do, but the rewards far exceed the effort of just shooting out a quick text or Facebook message. Since they failed miserably at Recallability, it brought both their Likeability and Credibility down. It made me question their authenticity and professionalism.

PINGING

There is a saying that "short visits make for long friendships." One of my favorite books for networking advice is the book *Never Eat Alone* by Keith Ferrazzi. In it he used the word "pinging," which means to stay in touch with your network. He says you can text, call, or do anything that reconnects you to someone else. He calls it a ping because it is simple a way to stay in touch with someone and increase your Recallability.

My friend Dan McCormick is the best example of someone who pings and is one of the most successful network marketers in the world. He is always asking questions:

"How's your family? How was your trip that I saw on Facebook? How is business? What's the latest in your life?"

As I have spoken to many other of his friends, I found out that this is just who Dan is. He is a professional pinger. I consider that a compliment. A professional pinger to me is someone who is really good about genuinely caring about others, so good that they always find a way to stay in touch. I recently just got back from a networking conference. Somehow, while talking to a 30-year veteran in network marketing, Dan's name was brought up. The first thing said was, "Oh you know Dan! He is amazing. He still calls me every few months and has done so for 20 years." While his pinging ways may seem unconventional, so is the fact that he is a multi-millionaire.

Professionals do the little things that the average person doesn't do over and over again, and Dan's ability to become a professional pinger has helped him become the successful man he is today. Many of your old acquaintances have probably now become almost strangers. Not total strangers, but you probably wouldn't feel comfortable asking them for anything, nor would they feel comfortable asking you for anything. They aren't part of your network. People aren't strangers if you stay in contact with them. That doesn't even mean a regular phone call. The trick is to stay in contact with them before you need their help. Think of pinging as a tune-up with your friends. You need to take care of your friends just like you need to change the oil in your car every three months.

Just like the last example with Dan, it takes time to foster relationships that can prove to be fruitful when you need them the most. If you aren't making regular deposits into your emergency savings account, don't be surprised when you desperately need to make a withdrawal and you aren't able to do so. Do you honestly make regular deposits into your relationships, or only when it's convenient for you? Again, the best time to network is when you don't need anything. When everything seems to be going well, you don't need anything, and your urgency to network is low; that should be a flashing neon sign telling you that you need to network and care for your relationships.

GRATITUDE

*The deepest craving of human nature is the need
to be appreciated.* —William James

You typically don't think of gratitude as a principle to help you with recallability, but it is a very dynamic vehicle for increasing it. Gratitude is one of the best ways to make others feel important and connected to you. Lack of appreciation is one of the top reasons for someone quitting their job. It is certainly one of the most common answers I receive when I ask people why they are leaving their current company. I am not talking about the newbie network marketer who leaves for various reasons. I am referring to those who are really committed and who have been with their current company for at least a year.

Zig Ziglar always talked about maintaining an attitude of gratitude. I know that when I am in a bad mood, I am never in an attitude of gratitude. When I am in a good mood, I can usually find tons of things to be grateful for. One of the fastest ways to change your mood from bad to good is to think of some things you are grateful for: the bed you sleep in, the clean air you breathe, your good health, a loving family, knowing where your next meal is coming from. Little things that we often take for granted every day can instantly put you in a state of gratitude if you really take the time to think about them.

CHAPTER 6

BECOMING
UNFORGETTABLE

Staying in touch with people and displaying an attitude of gratitude can sometimes be difficult. Here are some strategies you can start implementing right away to help get ahead and stay organized.

1. MASTER ADDRESS LIST

I have a Google Doc that I update regularly. I keep all significant friends, family members, or associations' addresses there. You can use this to send out thank you cards, simple gifts, and holiday cards. People tend to like people they relate with, but they also tend to like people who both like them and who are thoughtful. Holiday cards are a simple way to be thoughtful of others.

2. THANK YOU TEXTS, CARDS, AND CALLS

Thank you, thank you, thank you! It goes a long way. After every first meeting with anyone, I always send a thank you text. Many times I continue to do it even after I have gotten to know the individual.

3. GRATITUDE JOURNAL

A gratitude journal is meant to help you reflect on all the positive things in your life and put yourself in a positive state of gratitude. You can be creative with this. You could write one thing you are grateful for in your life and one thing you are grateful for in your business. There's really no wrong way to do a gratitude journal, unless you're not doing one at all.

4. THE GRATITUDE CHALLENGE

Try calling or even sending one text a day thanking someone for something they have done, either recently or in the past. It's a difficult habit to get into, but it's totally worth it. Try doing it at a set time every day to get into a habit. Do it for a week, then that turns into a month, and next thing you know, you've sent gratitude texts for a year or more!

5. FIGURE OUT WAYS TO RECONNECT

"When two people exchange dollar bills, each still only has one dollar. When two people each exchange networks, they each have access to two networks," according to Harvey McKay. When two people exchange dollar bills, each person is providing something of value, but no significant gain or loss has occurred. Instead, the transaction builds a sense of trust. You must keep reconnecting with others to build that trust and stay recallable. By understanding the value of exchanging networks it will give you a deeper purpose to want to reconnect.

People love to be remembered. Find ways to send a text of a good memory, an inquiry of how they are doing, an invitation to connect on the phone soon to catch up, and/or a congratulations on any recent achievement. Honestly it could be anything but if the relationship means anything to you it shouldn't be too hard to find a reason to reconnect.

THE FRIENDSHIP FORMULA SIMPLIFIED

Authors Jack Schafer & Marvin Karlins talk about the friendship formula in their book *The Like Switch*. I think it is a great formula to help you not only build your relationships but also to better understand the different levels of Recallability. They have found that proximity, frequency, duration, and intensity are the four factors that strengthen a friendship. Studying and implementing these four factors really are part of the formula to stronger friendships. Think of these four factors as the best principles for improving Recallability:

Proximity is how close you are to a person. This doesn't always have to be physically close, especially with video chatting technology nowadays. However, spending some quality one-on-one time together will do more for a relationship than hanging out in a group.

Frequency refers to how often you spend time with someone. Do you talk to this person once a month? Once a week? Every day? As the frequency goes up, the quality doesn't always have to be as high. If you and your spouse see each other every day, then there is no need to go on date night every single night. However, if your spouse is part of the military and comes home for two weeks before having to be deployed again, you are going to make sure that those are an incredible two weeks because the frequency of seeing that person is lower. The more often you are around someone, the more they will trust you. In marketing and advertising, you are taught that it takes a consumer seven times of seeing your ad before they buy. This same principle relates for building trust with others. Increase the frequency to increase the trust.

Duration is the length of time that you are spending with someone. If you run into a friend while shopping at the mall and just say hello while passing by, while it's better than nothing, it will do very little to build that relationship. However, if you organize a time to go out with that same friend, even in a group, the relationship will be better just because you spent more time with that person.

Lastly, intensity is the key to the vault. This is all about quality instead of quantity. It is about connecting with people at a personal level over simply collecting names. Intensity is like the culmination of the previous three factors: proximity, frequency, and duration. If you are close to someone often and spend long amounts of time with that person, you are going to naturally have a greater relationship with that person than someone you barely see. If the frequency you are around a person is low, the duration you spend with them must obviously be high. Muhammad Ali said, "Don't count the days, make the days count."

I love that quote from Muhammad Ali and to make it my even deeper I would say, "Don't count the moments; make the moments count!"

The more time you spend around someone, the more influence you have. When working on maintaining relationships, it is important to remember this! It might sound more difficult to organize a time to go to lunch with someone to catch up, but it will be a lot more meaningful and beneficial in strengthening the relationship than an occasional text, phone call, or chat while in passing will ever be because that is implementing multiple factors from the Friendship Formula.

NETWORK LIKE A PROFESSIONAL!
SOCIAL MEDIA STRATEGIES TO CRUSH RECALLABILITY

Social networking is brilliant.
Just when you think it's doom and gloom
and you have to spend millions of pounds on marketing
and this and that, you have this amazing thing
now called fan power.
The whole world is linked through a laptop.
It's amazing. And it's free.
I love it. It's absolutely brilliant. — Simon Cowell

Let me get to some strategies you can and should start implementing today to network like a professional. If you don't consider yourself very good at social media this will be the most overwhelming part of the book. Take a deep breath. You don't need to know everything. Read this entire section first. Then pick one section to implement. I do feel strongly that social media is becoming so relevant in everything we do that I need to spend a little more in depth on this particular topic.

We have gone over first impressions. Many first impressions nowadays actually come from social media. People literally decide who you are or aren't based on your social media content. We all know that social media is a huge part of our lives, but I don't think most of us truly realize just how much potential there is with it. Through social media, you are able to know what's going on in someone's life. We can reach 60 people in 60 different countries in 60 seconds using our thumbs. There is no way you can build a brand and maintain the trust of a vast majority of people without social media. As professionals, it is imperative we are using social media correctly to network!

Calvin Becerra has spent years building his brand the right way. He is all over social media giving a great balance of who he is as a leader, husband, father and friend. He is a personal friend and I am amazed at how well he does on social media portraying who he really is. He will give insightful leadership posts mixed with lifestyle and family. As you follow Calvin on social media you are attracted to his brand which represents him very well. Find others to follow to learn how to brand yourself. As always, just be the best version of you, but always learn from other top leaders.

Now this book isn't going to provide a total and complete social media breakdown, but there are a couple small things I want to share with you that will help you grow your brand and Credibility on the internet.

First off, make sure to post at least once a week. Share something of value. Sometimes it could be about your personal life, while other times it could be something funny or inspiring. I think you should be doing at least two posts per day, but I know everyone can do at least one post per week. If you want to be a good leader and networker there's no excuse to not be putting your own insightful stuff out there into the ocean of social media!

As your posts get better, they will be shared and you will build an audience that expects you to share your insights. One of my friends started posting his morning insights every day. Eventually he started posting 2 to 3 times a day. He is very insightful and now has close to 200,000 followers. The first year he didn't get much traction at all, but he kept at it. His insight got better, as did his following. Some of his posts are now shared over 1,000 times. Whether it is to your face, or behind your back, you will get a ton of criticism at first. Deal with it. Learn from it. Push through it. Stop worrying about all of the people who won't ever help build your dreams and focus instead on those who respond to your content.

Keep in mind the ultimate goal: you are seeking connections that lead to real relationships! The more connections you have, the happier you will be and the more success you will have. The stronger those connections are, the more your happiness and success is amplified.

I always try to stay in contact with my top 20 best contacts every two weeks. A lot of times my inner circle rotates people in and out, but I always make sure to have at least 20 of my best contacts who are not a part of my network marketing business that I stay in touch with at least every other week. If someone came to your mind, but you feel like it would be more like a chore to reach to out every two weeks, then that person probably doesn't belong in your inner circle!

I know this may sound repetitive, but as you know, your goal is to find a way to serve and provide more value to these 20 contacts than you receive. Don't focus on using them or you have failed miserably! Focus on how you can help them. If you provide value with the right intentions, you will be rewarded. It may not even be directly by one of those 20 contacts. It could come from your association from them. It could come from you becoming a better person by providing more value for others. I really don't know where exactly the value will come directly from but I can promise you that the universe will conspire to help you. I am not someone who typically throws out phrases like 'the universe will conspire to help you' but there is no other way to better explain this principle.

The most important principle to accomplishing our success is asking ourselves "How can I help enough people to get what they want?" "How can I serve with no expectation but to serve?"

Building a positive, selfless, servant driven relationship with our distributors is important. In fact, it's so vital that if we ignore it, we won't be able to sustain anything that we build. We'll always be pushing the boulder up the steepest of mountains, wishing, hoping and praying. —James Yates

There are going to be people who read this book and say, "Wow, great book! That was insightful." There are also going to be people who actually take these principles and put them into action. I am about to tell you one of those little things I do that makes me a disciplined networker, so take notes and be ready to implement this into your lifestyle as well!

In a world where it's so simple to just send out a direct message on social media or draft a quick text, you have to take the time to do something that so few people do: Just stay in contact! A few times a year I go through all of the contacts in my phone. I try and send texts out to those I haven't been in contact in a while just to keep up with our relationship. I know this sounds so simple, but I promise if you just stay in contact a few times a year, you will make a tremendous impact.

Casey Eberhart is a keynote speaker, trainer, business strategist, and an expert in networking. He gives a ton of relevant and updated info on networking. I met Casey at a networking event where we were both speaking. He listened to my speech on networking and immediately we connected and shared with each other our insights on how to better network. He pointed out that he reaches out to 10 people a day to just connect with them. He makes no mention of business. He focuses on being a good friend.

If nothing else, try to make sure you have every contact in your phone added on some social media platform, like Facebook. This way, even if you aren't sending them direct text messages more than once or twice a year, they can continue to keep up with your life indirectly through social media, and they will feel closer to you, even if you haven't personally talked in a while. I have so many friends on social media that I feel like I know so much about them, even though I haven't had a good conversation with them for a while!

If you want to knock out a few birds with one stone, start a group text. Obviously you can't just lump people together and take the lazy way out, because you'll do more harm than good if you do that. Each of your group texts needs to be centered around a specific niche group. Maybe you play golf with some friends, that could be one group. Maybe you go to church and always find yourself running into the same two or three families that know each other, that could be another group. Maybe you had really great relationships with some friends back at school that you've lost touch with, it's time to bring the group back together! Maybe you have a group with your favorite sports team. Find ways to reconnect with people.

You don't want to overkill your group messages, and there are times where it may be better to text an individual rather than lumping someone in a group, but that is a judgment call. Group texts or messages are a lot of fun, and a great way to stay involved with multiple people at once.

In a recent article network marketing rock star Amber Voight said this about her social media strategy:

> You need to become influential. You do this by bringing
> value to other people's lives. You make friends with lots
> of other networkers and direct sellers, and then post
> things to help them, even if they're not in your company.
> Rather than post about my business, I share general

network marketing tips and inspirational quotes or videos,
because that's going to help people grow, and as they
grow, their business grows. It will come back to you, but
some people just don't get that part. They think, 'How
can I benefit if they're not even in my company?' The
Universe always rewards you, often in unforeseen ways.

John and Nadya Melton always show a great balance of business tips, humor, and real life on their social media. Every time a new friend adds John or he adds a new friend, he always sends a voice memo through Facebook messenger. The fact that John takes that time with every new personal contact is phenomenal. I love that he sends out voice memos, as it makes it more personal. Very few even take the time to say hello to their new contacts, let alone make it personal with a voice memo. John takes it a step further and will reach out consistently to his contacts. For years, I hadn't personally met John, but due to his social media posts and our back and forth voice memos, I always felt like I personally knew him. These are some of the ways John and Nadya separate themselves from most network marketers.

There are some common threads that run through all these stories of successful and inspirational social media marketers. In order to better understand them, I encourage you to find several people with solid engagement and follow them. Study them. What do they post? How often do they post? What type of content do they post? Remember to find your style and that followings aren't built overnight. They take time!

In large part, social media will become your resume, so keep it polished! Make sure that your profile picture is sharp. This is the first thing someone scrolling through your profile will see. Your picture should be high quality and convey your message—do you want to be seen as fun, successful or family-oriented? Additionally, depending on which social media format you are on, there may be a section to fill out about yourself. Keep it simple, yet profound. Be brief on who you are and what you are interested in.

There are so many different social media platforms out there, and I'm not going to pretend to be a master at every one. I know it can be overwhelming, so start with one and master it. Then move on to the next. Take a deep breath. You don't have to learn all of these at once. In fact, many top industry leaders only master one of these platforms. So start with one, then you can decide if you would like to add more.

CURRENT RELEVANT PLATFORMS FOR
NETWORK MARKETING

*Networking is marketing. Marketing yourself,
marketing your uniqueness, marketing what you
stand for.* — Christine Comaford-Lynch

Now that we've established how to use social media and its importance, let's quickly run through current platforms. Social media is constantly changing, so my main objective is to teach you principles that are timeless to help you adapt.

FACEBOOK

Facebook is currently by far the most popular social media platform; over 70% of the adult population uses it. It is definitely the best platform for increasing awareness of your brand. Due to its use in just about every business and social function, it is still a social media platform that has lots of value and is worth learning how to use correctly.

- Facebook Posts with a photo generate 120% more engagement than simple text.
- Posts shorter than 250 characters have 60% more engagement than longer posts.
- Posts on Thursday and Friday have 18% better engagement rates than other days of the week.
- Posting a question doubles the engagement over non-question posts.
- Videos typically get more engagement than photos do.
- According to Panorama Emoticons receive 33% more comments, are shared 33% more often, and are liked 57% more than Facebook posts without emoticons!

Here is my scoring for how well I am doing on Facebook: if someone shares your Facebook post, that is worth the most. Sharing your content is the ultimate compliment; it gets the most amount of new eyeballs seeing your brand or audience — 30 points for each share. Yes, that's a ton of points, but shares are that valuable!

Others commenting on your posts is also very worthwhile, as that indicates your post was worthy of someone taking the time to say something about it. I give four points for each comment.

Someone liking your posts is worth one point. Likes are still worthwhile, and a compliment, but if you get shares, you almost always get additional likes and comments. If you get comments you almost always get likes, but if you just get likes, you may or may not get shares or comments.

Another thing I've noticed is that videos get more engagement than pictures and posts. I don't have a score yet for views on videos, but I do track and monitor how many views I get on each video I post. I admit, videos were really uncomfortable for me at first. I am not someone who strives for attention, so it was very awkward. I felt like a complete idiot on my first ten videos or so, but the more videos I filmed, the more comfortable I became. I was able to re-watch my videos and see where I screwed up.

Recently, I posted a video that I thought was awful. In fact, I almost considered not posting it. I personally thought the previous five videos were better, but I decided to just post it anyway. Of course, it ended up being the most liked video of the last six videos that I posted! I say "of course" in my most sarcastic tone. You just never know what will relate to others. I have had so many posts that I thought would do really well and they haven't, and I have had so many posts that I thought would be awful and they ended up being very popular.

A simple comment on someone's post goes a long way. I know it sounds silly, but trust me when I say it makes a big difference. Commenting on Facebook is a huge step towards building both trust and Likeability. Those who share, comment, and like your posts are your most loyal followers. Treat them right! Comment back. Follow back. Reciprocate the love! Engage others in your posts by replying to their comments, liking their comments, and asking questions every so often in your post. I like to say things like, "Do you agree? What am I missing? What are your thoughts? What's your opinion?" This creates a more loyal following, makes others feel important, and the additional comments help the Facebook algorithm so the amount of users that see your post increases.

Evan Klassen understands social media very well. He has created one of the best brands out there. Most people would never guess that I met him through his social media brand. After he commented on my social media posts, I wanted to reach out to him. I sent him a private message and we later connected at an event. Evan has now become a trusted friend, and it is all attributed to him commenting on my Facebook posts. Evan's social media advice is to pick one social media platform to learn well and become great at it.

There are some great features on Facebook that can help you organize your friends and make your use of social media more efficient. Let's say there is a person that posts content you absolutely love and you really don't want to miss any posts from them. Go to the profile of this superstar and in the drop down menu, you will see an option to make the person a "see first." This means that all of their posts will show up at the top of your news feed and you can follow them without much effort at all. I have a few close friends on Facebook, and I always get their updates. Instead of just grouping everyone on Facebook, using these little-known features can allow you to eliminate distractions and focus on what, or who, is important.

> *Instead of telling the world what you're eating for breakfast, you can use social networking to do something that's meaningful.* —Edward Norton

Make people feel a part of your posts. Social media is about connecting others to your life. It is about giving them insight into who you are. It is almost like you become a reality TV show. Make others feel connected.

STOP! Feeling overwhelmed yet? Take another deep breath. Remember you don't need to learn all of this. Read through this once and find that one part you want to implement.

Social media can be extremely effective, especially if used in a respectful manner. Use it to brand yourself. Use it to connect with people. Use it to build your business, but just use it the right way!

Okay, break time is over! Now back to learning more social media strategies.

> *When I hear people debate the ROI of social media, it makes me remember why so many business fail. Most businesses are not playing the marathon. They're playing the sprint. They're not worried about lifetime value and retention. They're worried about short-term goals.* —Gary Vaynerchuk

INSTAGRAM

Instagram is one of my favorite platforms. I love Instagram! It to me has a much more personal feel to it. It is simple—photos or video—and uses a lot less text. Unlike Facebook, when you comment on Instagram it won't automatically notify any of the others who commented (although there is an option to get post notifications from people you follow if you choose). Instagram Stories (similar to SnapChat) can also be immensely valuable if you use it correctly. It is definitely for the mobile-savvy generation and 57% of users access the site on a daily basis, mostly on their phones.

You get extra points for originality and sincerity. Don't post a similar picture three times. Yes you read that correctly. Many Instagram posters post a picture of their vacation or their kids several times in a row. They post almost identical photos! There is a balance between posting often enough but not too often. If you are posting five times a day, you better be a celebrity or you better be a business with a very specific niche or brand. Even still, I would recommend that you post anywhere from one to three pictures or videos per day. Also add witty captions, they always get props. The photo is obviously important but the caption can make all of the difference.

Instagram is also a platform perfect for reciprocation. If others follow you, there is a much higher chance that they will continue to follow you if you follow them back. It doesn't matter how much someone likes your content: unless you are a celebrity, if you don't follow them back they will be offended and typically stop following you. Respond to comments just as I taught you earlier in the Facebook section. You want to reward those who engage in your posts.

So which businesses should be on Instagram? Image-friendly businesses and businesses that want to appeal to younger demographics work best. As mentioned earlier, Instagram Stories are very similar to Snapchat, so I would recommend reading through the Snapchat section that follows to get a better understanding of the best way to use it. The principles are exactly the same.

Now, let's change the subject. Does anyone really like eating Spam? You know, the slimy processed meat in a can—no thank you! I guess if I had nothing left to eat and my life depended on it, it would be just fine. Most people, such as myself, believe that Spam should be kept as food storage for life-saving purposes only. Just as Spam is a last resort for food in emergency situations, net-spamming should be viewed in the same way for our businesses.

Net-spamming is not the same as networking. And net-spamming does not leave a good taste in your mouth, especially when received from a friend. Refrain from net-spamming your friends about what you're selling or needing from them on any social media, Facebook, Twitter, Instagram, LinkedIn, etc. Social networks are called social networks for that exact reason: they are meant to be socially engaging. If somebody wanted to sign up for spam networks like Spambook, Instaspam, Snapspam, or LinkedSpam, they just need to turn on the TV and watch commercials. How many people enjoy commercials nowadays? Exactly. Each social networking platform has a "block" and a "delete" button for a reason. Don't be the reason.

Our business model is so powerful, but an outsider may perceive us as nuts when we post constantly pitching our business! Posting about your business isn't wrong. I have been teaching you my social media strategies but let's have some fun. Let me show you some of what NOT to do regarding social media that'll make you laugh.

These are the top six people who drive me nuts on social media:

- *The Misplaced Twitter User*: "Just woke up." "I'm eating now." "What to do today?" "I'm stuck in traffic." "I feel like I have no friends." Really? You don't say? I wonder why that is?

- *The Self-Promoter*: When every post or every other post is promoting some sort of accomplishment or a throwback picture to glory days. When just about all of the comments are "Well done!" or "You're amazing!" or "So impressive," it is time to change up your posts. It's obvious when people fish for compliments or are humble boasting. Every so often is okay, just not constantly.

- *The TMIer*: "Jocelyne is headed to Walgreens to get something to fix her diarrhea, my poor baby": ("Um, wow. OK. I really would have been OK not knowing this"). Don't share private things in public. You and your significant other just had a fight? Trust me, the world does not want to know!

- *The Alluder*: "Hang in there Jamie, don't worry, your secret is safe with me!" That's not even alluding and usually people are more subtle than that, but you know what I'm talking about. Don't allude to things no one else knows because you think you are more important or a better friend. Maybe you do know more but stating it for everyone else to see just makes you look bad.

- *The Maddening Obscurist*: "Should I, or should I not?" "All things happen for a reason." No one knows what you're talking about! If you feel the need to just put little thoughts into the universe, get a journal. Don't be weird.

- *The Chronic Inviter*: Game requests. Petitions. Game requests. Quizzes. Game requests. Tests. Game requests. Group Invites. Game requests. Page invites. Game requests. Please, stop the madness!

SNAPCHAT, INSTA STORY AND FACEBOOK STORY

Snapchat, Instagram Stories and Facebook Messenger Day are very personal opportunities to show people more about what you do and why you do it. They all give their users so much freedom, from sending pictures and videos about 'their reality" to chatting via text or live video. You can let people into your personal life by letting them see what you're up to, anytime you can access your camera phone, which is just about any time. Personals snaps are like texting pictures to your friends, while adding snaps to your story is like adding photos or videos on your Facebook feed.

The engagement rate on Snapchat, Instagram Stories and Facebook Messenger Day is extremely high. They could be considered the most addictive of all the social media platforms. One of the major reasons people are engaging on these story-type platforms is the 24 hour time-limit on snaps. They will be gone forever, so you better not miss it! This fact also encourages more posting instead of limiting yourself like the other platforms. People snap about everything and anything because it disappears. All three of these story platforms can really let people see who you are as a person in everyday life. It's like your own reality TV show.

Snapchat, Instagram Stories and Facebook Messenger Day can be the perfect tools to build your brand. You are going to be able to share what your life is like with your friends, family, and followers. Whether you are focused on finding more customers or just promoting your business, your stories can share anything you want them to... and the crazy part is people will WATCH IT!

According to my good friend Dallin, this is what you NEED TO DO to be successful on a story:

- Allocate some time to learning the platform.
- Look at YouTube How-To Videos.
- Be real.
- Show your lifestyle daily.
- Be consistent.
- Don't start unless you are going to let people in on the ride.
- Provide value.
- Remember, content is King

Snapchat, Instagram Stories or Facebook Messenger Day could be a big asset this year to your brand this year. We are in the business of telling stories, and there is no more engaging way of telling them. Personally, I recommend you use one of the three consistently. Don't try to use all three or you will not build any of them. If you haven't yet focused on building any type of story platform on social media I would recommend you start where you already have the largest audience. For example, if you have the largest following on Instagram then you should be using Instagram Stories. If your following is the largest on Facebook, then you should be focused on building your daily stories on Facebook Messenger Day. Start where you have the largest following and then stay consistent.

WE ARE ALMOST THROUGH THE SOCIAL MEDIA SECTION!

If you aren't overwhelmed, then congratulations! If you are bored, then skip ahead past this section. If you are enthralled by this section, we have a few more platforms to cover.

Live Streaming is becoming more popular whether it be Facebook Live, Periscope, or whatever is the latest live streaming sensation. There is something about 'live' that makes it more genuine, real, and attractive. At the time of writing this book, live video streaming is still fairly new and not many people are using it. The ones that do use it currently do a great job at connecting with their audience. They take advantage of the platform by interacting with their viewers in real time, and that makes the viewer feel special.

It is also cool to watch a live streaming video because you get to see someone in real-time without having a fancy edited video to go along with it. It allows you to look into someone's real and raw lifestyle, and it makes that person seem more real. I would recommend going live at least once per week, even if it's only for five minutes.

I realize how uncomfortable it can be to do any live videos, let alone daily ones, so start with once a week and build up from there. At the beginning, don't be discouraged by the lack of views. It will take time to build an audience and polish your live skills. That's all part of the process that you must be willing to go through in order to become a professional. Be consistent in doing your live videos. Be authentic and do your best to have a concise message with a few simple steps. Lastly make sure to do live videos for the replay. Don't be constantly giving shout outs to everyone who joins. That will annoy the person who replays your video which will be the vast majority of your views. Don't wait for people to join your Facebook Live. Remember to do your Facebook Live with the replay viewers in mind. Don't waste time. Get started and get to the point.

People appreciate feeling connected to you, and you will build yourself up, almost as a celebrity, because of the effect that "seeing someone on TV" has on people. As always, watch others perform Facebook Lives to learn from them. Two of the people you should study are Billy Funk and Jessie Lee Ward. Jessie has that natural energy that attracts an audience but there is much more to her Facebook Lives than just her charisma. As you watch her closely, you will see specific techniques that she uses to engage her audience. She is constantly sharing personal stories and being very relatable. She is constantly asking her audience questions so that they actively engage in the comments section. This draws in the audience and will also gain you many more videos views. Billy, on the other hand, seems so quiet and reserved in normal conversation but you should see him on a Facebook Live. He also truly gets how to engage the audience. He creates great titles in his videos. He is well-prepared with his content and gives you a step-by-step process to implement. At times, he will even do crazy out-of-the-box things like wear a blue wig to grab your attention. His style may or may not be yours. That's not relevant. You should study anyone who is successful at engaging the audience on Facebook Live and learn the principles of what makes them successful. Then apply those principles to your own style and personality. Facebook Live is quickly becoming the most important branding tool in all of network marketing.

BLOG OR NEWSLETTER

While the act of blogging isn't actually considered part of social media, having a presence online that allows people to tap into your raw thoughts can be very valuable. Nowadays, people are all about transparency, and a blog can help you seem easier to understand. You will increase your visibility, frequency, and Credibility if you create solid content for your blog. Everyone looks people up on social media or in a Google search. If you aren't found on the Internet, you aren't credible. Get your content out there and distinguish yourself from the masses.

WordPress is free for blog creation and is very simple to learn. There are also many great websites that can help you create a newsletter. Having a consistent newsletter with your insight and content is just another powerful way to add to your brand.

STAND OUT

Social media can help you as an individual be your own brand by making your social media one big story. Being a storyteller pays big money. Steve Jobs was one of the world's greatest storytellers. He said, instead of simply delivering a presentation like most people do, he informed, educated, inspired, and entertained all in one presentation. Jobs once asked Pepsi then-president, John Sculley, "Do you want to spend your life selling sugar water or do you want to change the world?"

Differentiate yourself from the pack. Stand out! Disrupt comfort zones. "Ships in the harbor are safe... but that's not what they're built for." Become memorable! It doesn't take much, but it will make all the difference for you. Master the message. You can have the greatest idea in the world, but if you can't communicate your ideas, it doesn't matter. Social media is not your business, but it is an absolutely necessary asset to your business.

Remember, social media is constantly changing. During the course of writing this book over the past year there have already been three major changes in the social media world. My main goal with these lessons is to teach you the principles. As you learn them it is actually pretty easy to then adapt them. Until then it all can be quite overwhelming. Yet, while social media is very important to your business, it cannot replace verbal communication.

> *Technology is a compulsive and addictive way to live.*
> *Verbal communication cannot be lost because of a*
> *lack of skill. The ability to listen and learn is key to*
> *mastering the art of communication. If you don't use*
> *your verbal skills and networking, it will disappear*
> *rapidly. Use technology wisely.* — Rick Pitino

CHAPTER 7

THE LAW OF
PROFITABILITY

LAW #3.5

Does anyone know the story of one of the greatest mergers of all time? It was the 2006 Disney/Pixar merger which saved a struggling Disney. As the two companies were negotiating the merger in 2004, they came to a dead-end and it seemed as if the deal would never happen. From 2004 to 2006 they couldn't get a deal done because they failed to follow this last Law of Networking.

The two companies broke off talks due to a strained relationship between Steve Jobs and former Disney CEO Michael Eisner. When Bob Iger succeeded Eisner, he immediately extended an olive branch to Jobs. Within three months of taking over as CEO, Iger had created a seven-billion dollar merger that many believed to be too expensive. Both sides felt their value was extremely high, and both sides were right; but Bob Iger understood the win-win scenario that could be created between the two parties. He made a bold move that literally transformed a struggling Disney company and a moderately successful Pixar company to legendary status.

As of late 2017 Pixar has now released 17 movies, and ALL have grossed over 300 million in sales! Disney has quadrupled its stock since 2006 with a massive increase in their animation, which is a large part of their brand strategy. Their animation fuels their merchandise, cable TV, and theme parks.

But before going into detail about the last half-law of networking, I am going to give you my definition of The Law of Profitability. Simply, it is creating a win-win scenario. That's it. Think bigger than just money, although sometimes it is money that creates your win-win scenario. For some a win-win isn't the money, it's the association or mentorship.

Here is a super simplified formula to being successful. The Law of

Profitability is only a half-law because it is all about putting the three Laws we already covered into action. My Strategy to implement this law is:

- Read 30 books a year (Learn).
- Go to lunch or dinner with 70 different people a year (Likeability and Recallability).
- Take action in your profession (Credibility).

Do this, all out, for five years, and I believe you will be successful. I know it's pretty blunt and straight-forward, but I am almost certain that if you took action on the three things I just mentioned above, you'll be doing way more work than 99% of your competition are currently doing. In order to truly Network you must make sure you follow through with The Law of Profitability. You must focus on creating win-win scenarios. This is one of my simplified strategies. Your strategy may be a little different but I hope you understand the principles taught behind my strategy. I hope that you create your own strategy based on the taught principles.

THE ABUNDANCE MENTALITY

*I have an abundance mentality: When people
are genuinely happy at the successes of others,
the pie gets larger.* — Stephen Covey

In networking you are only as good as the value you provide to others. Sean Brady needs to change his middle name to abundance! He and his wife Cherrie are literally the true definition of abundance mentality thinking. Unfortunately, there are some leaders who talk about having an abundance mentality, but end up showing their true colors (like Jake the Taker) when a member of their team decides to leave and go to a new company. So many leaders may pitch that they have this mentality, but the second anyone leaves their company, you see their true colors. They start to bash that leaving team member, clearly showing that they actually have a scarcity mentality.

Sean has quite the story: he built a large network, lost it, and then rebuilt it all over again. He spent over a year in a foreign country, without his family, building his network marketing business. I don't have time to do his story justice, so I won't go into details. Sean literally cheers everyone on from every company. He offers to do three-way calls for other leaders in other companies to edify them. He begs to help crossline teams (where he has no financial gain) in any way that he can. He flies to many locations to do meetings where he has very little chance of financial gain and helps other team leaders. Sean is a flat-out winner who attracts the best of the best because he truly is the best kind of person there is. He doesn't just pitch the abundance mentality; he lives it every day! I strive to be more like Sean.

Both Sean and Cherrie taught me the value of karma over lunch at Malawi's Pizza in Provo, Utah. They taught me that the profitability principle isn't always about money. I was complaining to them about someone who had taken advantage of me in the business world. I was expecting both of them to feel sorry for me, but instead they taught me a powerful lesson.

They both shook their heads and told me how awful they felt for the person taking advantage of me. They went on to say that what goes around always comes around. They weren't worried about me. They knew I would be just fine if I kept abiding by the abundance mentality principle which, in the end, always leads to good karma. I learned at that moment that if you have the abundance mentality and focus on providing value for as many as you can, you will be fine. Don't worry about other's wrongdoings!

They taught me that understanding who you are and how you deal with others says a lot about you. They said they always focused on helping others to be successful, even if it didn't net them a dollar. Throughout their first five years of marriage, they were tested as they felt they were doing everything they believed was right, but it was not yielding the financial results they were looking for. It took them years of living the abundance mentality on a daily basis for them to see results. For the last 15+ years, they have lived a very successful lifestyle earning in excess of $15 million.

A huge insight that they didn't tell me, but that I learned from them is that compensation always catches up to skill set, abundance giving, and effort... but that it is almost always delayed. Their success hasn't stopped them from living what got them there. In fact, now they feel like they have more resources and time to live the abundance mentality more efficiently. I have seen countless examples where Sean meets an individual for the first time. He gives them his phone number and encourages them to call him for help. He has no hidden agenda with these individuals and assumes nothing financially will ever come out of it for him. He and his wife just believe that's how you should live your life. Sean and Cherrie view the profitability principle very differently from others and it has paid off in a major way.

I Helped a Competitor

Years ago I remember a friend named Mark Klassen came to me for advice on leaving his network marketing company. Naturally, if someone is leaving, you would love for them to join your company. You know your company the best. It benefits you and your team the most. I told Mark I would be more than happy to assist him in any way that I could. I asked him if he were open to checking out my current company. He kindly said he would keep an open mind but that it probably wasn't going to be a fit.

Sure enough, after checking out my company, Mark was proved right: my company was not a fit for him. I ended up giving Mark my opinion on several companies, and I connected him with other knowledgeable leaders in the industry to give him another opinion. I helped connect him with four different companies that I felt were solid, and he ended up choosing one. He has had a tremendous amount of success with his new company. I got no referral fee. I have not been, nor will I ever be, paid for those services, but I was simply following what I was taught: The Abundance Mentality. Do the right things for the right reasons. You will attract who you become. That encompasses Profitability.

The Law of Reciprocation

I have a good friend named Woody Woodward, the same Woody from the Lake Powell trip mentioned earlier in the book. Woody always asks, "What can I do to help you?" It's annoying because he is exactly what I am trying to be. I'm trying to be that guy that's always providing value to others, and this guy is so good at it that even when I feel that I am providing value to him, I'll know he'll find a way to one-up me! It's not a competitive thing, so much as it's just wired into his DNA.

He's trained himself to be a Giver instead of a Taker, and I feel so obligated to him because of that. I still feel that I always owe him. He is always thanking me. I don't even know how he finds so many things to thank me for, but his graciousness makes me feel important. He is always communicating with me and asking what else can he do to help me in business and life. Because of all the value that Woody has provided me, I know that if he ever needed my help, I would do anything possible to help him achieve his goal.

If you only network when you desperately need it, then you will be perceived by many as a Taker. Network marketers make this mistake often. Many network marketers have ruined friendships because of that Taker mentality. With the Taker mentality, it's as if all relationship-building practices go out the window the moment the Taker starts to prospect. It should be the exact opposite, because recruiting is all about building relationships! In network marketing, as soon as most people get a no, they instantly just move on to the next person. While you may not get any business out of a prospect the moment you prospect them, don't confuse moving on to the next person with discarding a relationship altogether.

GIVER VS TAKER

There are givers and takers in life. The takers eat well while the givers sleep well. Givers focus on providing value for others. Takers focus on what's best for them. One of my favorite books of all time is *Give and Take* by Adam Grant. This book studies how ambitious Givers typically start off slow but end up victorious at the end of the day. It makes sense! By focusing on others, you sometimes make perceived sacrifices but those sacrifices are like investments: you may be down a little bit of money right now, but it pays huge dividends in the long run. No one trusts a Taker. No one generally likes a Taker. Give more! Develop a relationship. Yes, it takes longer, but it's more successful.

Adam Grant looks at how some Givers that are too nice in the workplace end up at the bottom of the sales chart because they are not aggressive enough. Givers like that are on the brink of being fired for lack of productivity. It was also found that some Givers were also at the top of the sales chart, and they were usually over 50 percent higher than the Takers in the middle of the chart.

What does this mean? It means that Givers that don't know how to incorporate their own needs into the goals of others end up as chumps, while Givers that figure out how to incorporate their own needs with the goals of those they work with completely dominate the field. The Law of Profitability is Win-Win. Both sides must be taken care of for a deal to be successful. They are champs in every regard, and their Giver traits are a huge reason for their success.

The currency of real networking
is not greed, but generosity. —Keith Ferrazzi

MEET THE GIVER

*Giving connects two people, the giver
and the receiver, and this connection gives birth
to a new sense of belonging* — Deepak Chopra

Years ago I met this crazy optimistic dreamer. He had all of these crazy ideas. Right away, there was something about him where I just knew I could trust this guy. I could tell he was a Giver. I don't know if it was his charisma, how he spoke, or what he said, but you probably know that type of person. The person that you instantly know you can trust. This individual isn't just trustworthy; he is the "favor" guy. He is the guy that will do anything for anyone without anything in return. He is what I call an "Ambitious Giver."

Ambitious Givers provide so much value that they always win in the end. They also end up becoming super profitable in whatever they put their focus on, whether it be finances, relationships, growth, and more. The book *The Go Giver* is one of my favorite books of all time. It is all about how to become an Ambitious Giver. In summary, here is what I interpreted an ambitious giver to be, as taught in *The Go Giver*.

- Principle 1: *Value.*
  Give more than you take in income.

- Principle 2: *Compensation.*
  Your income is determined by how many people you
  serve and how well you serve them. If you want to be a
  billionaire, go serve a billion people. When you provide great
  value you will become a referral producing machine.

- Principle 3: *Influence.*
  Your influence is determined by how abundantly
  you place other people's interests first. People do
  business with people they know, like, and trust!

- Principle 4: *Authenticity.*
  The most valuable gift you have to offer is yourself.

- Principle 5: *Receptivity.*
  The key to effective giving is to stay open to receiving.

There may be times where some take advantage of Ambitious Givers, but it is rare to find someone who is so selfless and equally ambitious. This Ambitious Giver has given so much, that he is the go-to guy anytime you are looking for any sort of connection. Do you remember Brandon Carter who was mentioned earlier in the book? Let me refresh your memory. He helped Lance Conrad and me create a brand new initiative for a company that had $3 billion in lifetime sales. If you are going to start a business, you call an Ambitious Giver like Brandon Carter because everyone likes, respects, and trusts him. If you are looking for a job or a favor, or really anything at all, you always have someone like Brandon Carter at the top of your list. He provides so much value for so many that he has developed a huge network.

It pays big time to be an Ambitious Giver. Companies consistently seek Brandon's involvement because of his skillset, but even more so because of the strength of his trusted network. Your goal is to always strive to give more value to every person in your network compared to what they give you. One way to give is to help others out in any little way you can, such as random acts of kindness.

#RAK

*Service to others is the rent you pay for your room
here on earth.* — Muhammad Ali

With the advance of technology, we are aware now more than ever of how life is outside of where we live. We see starving, homeless people on TV, or we see in movies how those less fortunate are portrayed as helpless beggars. As people become more aware of how the rest of the world lives, that awareness has created more humanitarian efforts than ever before.

I believe that increased awareness has created millions upon millions of increased Random Acts of Kindness (RAK). I see countless YouTube videos and social media posts of simple Random Acts of Kindness go viral. It is very inspiring. One of the major successes in my time in network marketing is creating a cause. If your company has a cause you can get fully behind, do it. Otherwise, create your own cause for your group. It can't be a gimmick. You can't say one thing and do another. If you have a cause then you need to support it, recognize those who support it and have structure behind it.

I always had a desire to get fully behind something bigger than the business, something humanitarian-based. In 2013, Lance Conrad, Brandon Carter, and I, along with many others, decided to add that piece to our team. Every month, we would get together and go serve our communities. We weren't allowed to talk about business at all.

One month, we visited widows. Another month, we raised money for three fatherless families. I have had the good fortune of participating in all sorts of service projects, such as visiting sick kids, helping a pre-school clean up their whole play area, donating to food banks, raising money for the Oso, Washington mudslide, and more. Our goal is to attract the right like-minded people, and doing random acts of kindness will attract people that find that sort of activity desirable.

In network marketing, we attract leaders based on different variables; one of the major ways to attract leaders is by showing who you are as a person. The better the person you become, the more leaders you will attract. How amazing is that?! You make more money while becoming a better person. One of the things I love about this profession is that it is like a mirror reflecting all of your strengths and weaknesses.

Several times a year, my teams do Random Acts of Kindness blitzes. We challenge everyone to go do something to help out the world and brighten someone's day. I have had all sorts of different types of Random Acts of Kindness blitz days. I have done anything from paying for someone's gas or food to simply complimenting ten people in a day. It doesn't have to be about money, and it doesn't need to be complicated.

Help others and give something back.
I guarantee you will discover that while public service
improves the lives and the world around you, its greatest
reward is the enrichment and new meaning it will bring
your own life. — Arnold Schwarzenegger

A study published in 2009 in the Journal of Social Psychology talks about the science of giving back. Participants were asked to complete a life satisfaction survey measuring multiple factors of their happiness and gave them certain scores. The participants were then divided into three groups. The first group was instructed to perform a daily act of kindness for the next ten days. The second group was told to do something new every day for the next ten days. The third group received no special instructions. After the ten days had passed, all the participants were asked to take the same life satisfaction test. The first and second group experienced a significant boost in their happiness ratings, while the third group had no differences in their ratings.

If your team doesn't have something like this, they are missing out. You are missing out! Making money is great, but helping others and becoming a better person during that process is priceless. Every network marketing company claims to have the best compensation plan with the best products. Of course, both products and the compensation plan are foundational pieces of a solid company. However, these days, companies need more. They need culture. Culture and values are very important to people because they want to be a part of something good and uplifting. They want to make a difference and feel relevant. Using company success to serve and create a culture focused on doing good will differentiate a network marketing company from its competitors.

Not many people can raise $45,000 in one night, but Justin Prince did. Operation Underground Railroad has gathered the world's experts in extraction operations and in anti-child trafficking efforts to bring an end to child slavery. After watching a powerful video on the huge world problem of child trafficking and slavery, Justin felt compelled to not just watch, but actually do something about it.

I still remember getting a call from him inviting me to an early showing of the movie *The Abolitionist*, which shows real life extractions from Operation Underground Railroad. He was so passionate about helping out this cause. I would guess that 99 percent of the people in the theater weren't part of Justin's business. He didn't do it to build his business; he did it because he believed in the cause. He did it because it was the right thing to do, and he happens to be a very successful network marketer. This story illustrates one of the major reasons why people are attracted to who Justin is as a person. In this case profitability wasn't about making money; it was about becoming a better person.

Without a strong culture, your network will fail. Jordan Kemper's network marketing organization consists of more than 20,000 clients in 19 different countries. One of Jordan's greatest strengths is his ability to create a strong team culture. When speaking on culture, he gives the following insight, "when you are fighting for a cause greater than yourself you will always work harder."

Melyna Harrison was a millionaire from a business outside of the network marketing industry. She and her husband John had already made a lot of money before Melyna even began network marketing. She started with her network marketing company as a hobby where she could work with friends and help other people. She didn't need the money, so the purpose was deeper—to help others. When John had a drastic change at work, and the Harrisons lost just about all of their money, it was fortunate Melyna had already started with network marketing.

Now Melyna needed to replace her family's income. She had seen her husband work long hours for years only to have everything taken away. This also grew her motivation for her business. She was already deeply passionate about her company's products and how they could help others. Now she was passionate about getting her husband home and creating a residual income where her family could travel and create long-lasting memories. Melyna did it. She worked extremely hard and was able to bring her husband home, and he now helps her build their business.

Recently, Melyna and John decided to take their kids to Mexico for an entire month. What an experience! Without Melyna having that strong 'why' for her work, there is absolutely no way she would have been able to overcome all of the obstacles on her journey to success. Your struggle becomes part of your story, but only if you overcome that struggle. Your 'why' is what will get you through the struggle.

There is one quality which one must possess to win,
and that is definiteness of purpose,
the knowledge of what one wants, and a burning
desire to possess it. — Napoleon Hill

CHAPTER 8

MASTERING THE
WIN-WIN

How to Recruit Other Network Marketers

Don't let this section fool you. This is not going to be "Cross Recruiting 101." I am not going to teach you how to steal people from other companies for your own personal gain. That is selfish and a quality of a Taker, and you are not a Taker, you're better than that. You are a Giver. You make friends. You stay in contact. You provide value. You continue to build your Credibility. If people are ever looking to leave and start with a different company, they will call those they like and respect the most. Hopefully you!! You need to become that well-liked and respected person that people will come to when they are looking for change.

When recruiting others, I don't ever target companies. I don't ever target leaders. I don't buy or call downline lists of other companies. I always tell each leader that is brought to me from another company that if they are happy where they are, then I support them and would love to just connect with them. If they are unhappy with their current situation and open to learning from me, then I will provide value however I can to educate them. If they tell me they are happy where they currently are, I leave it at that! Don't pester someone to the point where they don't want anything to do with you. I don't connect with them just to try to slide in little remarks about how amazing our team is and indirectly recruit them. That is what Takers do, and you and I are better than that!

It's important you adopt an abundance mentality. Everybody pay attention to this: there is enough to go around! You don't need to target other companies or leaders. Yes, it is true that there is a chance that 'Double Blue Star Diamond Ambassador Executive Director Legend' leader XYZ will switch companies someday. If it happens, it happens. If they do switch companies, do you think they just decided to randomly drop out and become a network marketing free agent? No! They went to someone beforehand and made a game plan to make sure their team was in the best position to succeed.

There is not a chance in the world that desperately messaging and talking to someone will get them to want to partner up with you. That is what Takers do, and, once again, you and I are both better than that. You needed to have established that relationship and connection before they announced they were switching companies. Then they might have come to you when searching out new options. If you would have been a Giver, then you would have at least been in the running.

Make friends without a hidden agenda. Don't be a hyena waiting to attack when the moment is right. Learn from each other. It will build both your Credibility and theirs because you will both talk positively throughout the industry about the other. If that leader ever switches, and you've built a good enough relationship with them before they make the decision to switch, then of course they will call you. However, that should never be the focus or reason you make friends with another leader.

Remember, there are plenty of other ambitious leaders who have never been a part of the network marketing or Multi-Level Marketing industry. If you are new and still aren't sure what Multi-Level Marketing really means here is the simple definition. Multi-level Marketing, or MLM, is a system for selling goods or services through a network of distributors. Some call it network marketing while others call it MLM. Both have the exact same meaning. Len Clements is an incredible network marketing leader and is also like the Wikipedia of info for the network marketing industry. Years ago he wrote an article on MLM (Multi-Level Marketing) pirates.

A pirate is an old term used in the network marketing industry that describes a distributor who purposely targets other companies' distributors. Pirates see someone else's large body of work (large organization) and want to somehow take that group at all costs into their new group. Pirates are always looking for the shortcut. In Len Clemens article he said the following about MLM pirates: They aren't doing the industry any favors either. MLM needs new blood. We must increase our numbers by attracting more professional people from outside our little world. One of the reasons why it just hasn't happened (yet) might be the way this industry feeds on itself. We, in general, seem content to just keep recycling the same people over and over and over, until they drop out. For the most part, those entering MLM for the first time just enter the same cycle along with everybody else. And the number of new people coming in isn't exceeding those going out by much.

How to Handle Network Marketers
Who Leave Your Organization

Michael Jordan is considered the greatest NBA player ever. In college, he was highly recruited and ended up with The North Carolina Tar Heels. One of the greatest rivalries in all of sports is the North Carolina Tar Heels and the Duke Blue Devils. Mike Krzyzewski is the coach of the Blue Devils and is the college coach with the most wins in college basketball history. His famous nickname in the sports world became Coach K. He was early on in his career when he lost the recruiting battle for the great Michael Jordan. I would expect a coach young in their career, losing a recruiting battle to a rival, to be a little immature or at the very least to not reach out to his lost recruit. Coach K had the maturity to handle the loss of a recruiting battle. On October 29th, 1980 Coach Mike Krzyzewski wrote the following letter to Michael Jordan.

Dear Mike,

I am sorry to hear that you no longer have interest in learning more about Duke University however I do want you to know that my staff and I wish you the very best in your college career. You are a fine young man and you make an immediate impact on whatever you choose.

Take care, and best of luck.

Sincerely
Mike Krzyzewski
Head Basketball Coach

This letter blew me away. Coach K was a true networker at the very beginning of his coaching career. It is by no accident that he has had so much success.

Sometimes, things don't go your way. Sometimes, people leave your business. Sometimes people leave your network marketing organization. It happens! It is part of the business, and it will happen to you many times once you have a large networking organization. The majority of companies and distributors claim to have an abundance mentality. They claim that they only want what's best for you and always have your best interest no matter what. Unfortunately, many leaders fail to live by what they teach. The moment you leave their organization, your so-called "friendship" changes immediately. This is not true of all leaders by any means, but it does happen way too often.

In a normal job, when someone leaves to go to another company, it typically isn't that big of a deal. In network marketing, if you are a leader and leave to another company, it is a huge deal! This is a relationship business, so companies and distributors take it very personally. Not only do they take it personally, but it also directly affects their income. When you mess with someone's income, for the short-sighted fear sets in and emotions run high. You may also find yourself dealing with the 'Telephone Game' where someone says one thing, who tells someone else, who tells someone else, and before you know it, there are major untrue rumors flying around. When you mix hurt feelings with money, that is a recipe for disaster!

Here is my take. If anyone (leader or not) leaves your organization, it is because of one of these reasons:

1. You did a poor job leading them.
2. They found a better fit.
3. They made a mistake leaving.

The important part is that it doesn't matter! They are gone from your company, so do the right thing and part on good terms. Remember not to burn bridges. Be a good friend. Communicate with each other effectively so you can end on a good note and continue the relationship. Be who you said you were!

I personally don't feel that I lose leaders very often, and it is obviously hurtful when it happens. Yet, when you have a large organization it is inevitable. Every single time a leader leaves my group, I call them to wish them the best of luck. And I mean it.

I remember years ago a very sharp woman who had only been part of my team for a few months left for another company. I called her and told her that if she ever needed any mentorship or anything at all to not hesitate to call me. She broke down in tears and thanked me. It was a hard thing to do, but it was the right thing to do. It felt so gratifying that I was thinking bigger than just myself. This isn't always easy to do. I will admit that sometimes this is the last thing I want to do, but it is the right thing to do. Sometimes you will feel that you have done everything right and the other person is being impossible. My advice to you is to take a step back when you feel your ego may be getting involved and ask the question... how does it help?

An interesting side to this story, and a note of irony, is that I thought this girl was making a massive mistake leaving my team and company. She ended up having a tremendous amount of success and has been with her current company for eight years. Remember, serving others isn't about you, it's about the other person. A leader with a true abundance mentality realizes that the relationship, the happiness of the other person, and not the money is what real wealth is made of.

EGO = Eliminating Growth Opportunity

I recently saw a t-shirt that summed it up best: "Your ego is not your amigo." You should always be looking at how you can help others. If your ego comes into play and clouds your judgment, are you really helping others? How can you become a better leader and person? Take the high road no matter what! Don't let your ego get in the way of your happiness, your relationships, and your profitability. By taking the high road, even when it's tough, your ego will shrink and your happiness, quality relationships, and profitability will grow.

Being in the industry full-time since 2008, I have had thousands upon thousands of customers and distributors. As I said earlier, it is inevitable that leaders will leave your team. Five individuals—Bruno Morini, Josh Rapkin, Darren Olayan and Ryan and Ashleigh Di Lello—were all once leaders in my organization. I recently spoke to Josh on the phone, went to dinner with Ryan and Ashleigh, and am once again working with Bruno. Things don't always end up the way they did with Bruno and me, but with good intentions, great communication, a friendship-first attitude, and an abundance mentality, it is absolutely possible. I had no idea that Bruno and I would someday work together again, but, it didn't matter. Doing the right thing for the right reason is justification enough. Relationships are king when networking. Remember, only Takers burn bridges.

Travis and Summer Flaherty are two of the top industry leaders. They do a phenomenal job of staying mature when a distributor leaves their organization. I remember talking to Travis at length about the topic of how to handle it with maturity when your group leaves. He shared a story about a very large team in Peru that had left his organization due to some unforeseen problems. They were attached to Travis and Summer as leaders, but the company wasn't working out for this particular group. Travis said that when he visits Peru, his old team picks him up at the airport to hang out as friends, even though they are in a different company! That is network marketing done right!

One of the top leaders in network marketing, Tom Chenault, said it best: "Love like crazy, and then love more."

CONCLUSION

Do you remember Hans from the movie *Frozen*? Please don't be a Hans! I have two daughters, so I have seen the movie too many times. Hans is a Prince who upon arriving in the kingdom, Arendelle, makes an instant connection with Princess Anna. He uses every skill from Likeability and Credibility to manipulate his way into an engagement after only knowing Princess Anna for a whopping whole day!

Later in the movie, his true colors are revealed: his only intentions were to take over the kingdom, and he had no real genuine interest in Princess Anna. Kristoff on the other hand wasn't great at making a first impression, but he was truly a great guy who had Princess Anna's best interest. In the end, the tortoise (Kristoff) beat out the hare (Hans). Remember, intentions matter. Doing the right thing well, for the wrong reasons, is still the wrong thing! Fortunately, most of the skills from this book cannot be faked, and some are impossible to manipulate. Even still, please don't be a fake person like Hans!

WHO WINS IN NETWORKING: THE SPRINTER OR THE MARATHON RUNNER?

This profession isn't a marathon or a sprint. It is a bunch of races, some short, some long. If you always perceive this profession as a marathon, then you will never have a sense of urgency. If you always perceive this profession as a sprint, you will burnout. Sometimes, the situation requires us to sprint. When it's time to sprint, sprint really, really hard. When it's time to walk, walk with your chin up and be aware of your surroundings, because you never know when it may be time to start jogging or sprinting again.

The Deer, the Dog, the Giraffe and the Wolf

Lon Wardrop has had the single greatest impact on my network marketing career than anyone else. Without him I wouldn't be in this incredible profession. I still have his voice in my head coaching me. I have to share one of my favorite lessons from Lon with you. He used to always tell me there are four different types of animals in this business. I remember them distinctly because he wouldn't just tell the story, but he would act it out with impersonations of each animal. Now, these are just analogies, so please don't get offended. There are no bad intentions in this analogy and I know each type also has a ton of strengths that aren't mentioned.

Dogs get all excited about a new opportunity. They are going to conqueror the world! They run around and are so excited to show everyone their excitement. In fact, they get so excited that they pee on themselves and over everyone else around them! Unfortunately, as soon as things get tough for dogs they whimper and go off to lick themselves in the corner, taking themselves out of the picture.

Deer think they are faced with too many choices. Instantly fear begins to set in, and very soon when the deer gets a rejection it becomes like a car at night with headlights: the deer gets stuck when the headlights show up. You would think or assume they would simply just dart out of the road, but they get run over (thus the statement 'a deer in the headlights'). The deer has taken itself out of the picture.

Giraffes, as we all know, are very tall. On average, a full-grown giraffe is 14 feet tall. Giraffes get excited about a new challenge but don't jump all in. They are very strategic, and even more curious. In fact, they are so curious that they use their height and looooooong neck to continually peek over and check out what's going on, but don't leap in. They are the lookie-loos that never jump into action, thus taking themselves out of the picture.

Wolves are laser-focused. When wolves are excited, they have a look in their eyes of unwavering confidence. They are well-respected because they are never off their game and they exude self-respect. Wolves network well and travel in packs to make things happen. The packs they travel with are lifted up and perform better because of the consistency and leadership of the wolf. Unlike the dog, the deer, and the giraffe, the wolf does not take itself out of the picture because it refuses to conform and it creates its own reality.

Kierston Kirschbaum has over 50,000 distributors in her organization. She has the wolf mentality and says it best. "When we choose things that seem scary that's when we grow the most. Feel the fear and do it anyway."

Every decade we have some kind of economic downturn. Economies predictably go up and down. Individuals constantly switch occupations. The job market constantly changes. Quite a while back, it appeared to be impossible that Blockbuster would go bankrupt, yet it happened. Circuit City also seemed to have a solid revenue stream but also went out of business. Businesses change and new aptitudes are required.

Your best protection strategy is forever your NETWORK. Your NETWORK isn't just those individuals in the current network marketing business you're building. Your NETWORK is everyone you strive to build relationships with, and those they are connected to and so on, regardless if they are in your current company or not. Ability alone won't spare you. Not even education, nor the government, will spare you. A NETWORK is your best protection and is your best insurance policy. Networking is not only your insurance policy, it is the key to happiness. Networking is the foundation of life.

Be the best you. You can't be Steve Jobs! Richard Branson would have been horrible had he tried to be Steve Jobs. Steve Jobs would have been awful had he tried to be Richard Branson. They both have had an insane amount of success, but both of them did so because they focused on becoming a better version of themselves.

I have learned so much from so many great people in my life, but the most influential have been my wife Janeia, my parents, my first mentor in the industry Lon Wardrop, my brother and sister, and my business partner Lance Conrad. My mom taught me gratitude. My dad taught me to have belief in myself. Lon and Lance taught me boldness. My wife keeps teaching me how to treat others. She is the best person and networker I know.

I am so grateful for network marketing. I have had the great opportunity to not only grow a skill set but to continue to create so many long-lasting relationships. Networking has made me a better husband, father, leader, and friend. If I made no money at all, the amount of friendship and personal development that I have received alone would be worth it. No one tells you on their deathbed that they wish they would have been wealthier. Happiness truly is about the strong relationships we develop in this life.

What's going to make you different? Who are you, to yourself? Who are you to others? What do you want to be known for? Everyone says they are different, and that is true. However, you need to take it to the next level to stand out. What is going to make you exceptional?

There is very little that separates the good from the great. There are many things that you are good at, and a small number of things you are great at. I hope this book has helped you better understand the Game of Networking and the importance networking plays in every aspect of your life. I also hope that by applying these skills you can take your networking skills from good to great. Find one thing in this book that you can apply and go become a better networker today.

If you like this book, then please share it with your network. Start networking with someone else by gifting them a copy of this book. If you love this book, please leave a review on Amazon (www.tgonbook.com) and help me network. Leaving a review is something so simple but very few actually do it. I would greatly appreciate any reviews to help me with The Law of Credibility. If you do so please find me on Facebook and send me a screenshot of your review so I can thank you. If you hate this book, please send me your critique and let me know how I can improve it. Lastly, remember to join my Facebook group The Game of Networking so I can stay connected with you.

When you are in the final days of
your life, what will you want?
Will you hug that college degree in the walnut frame?
Will you ask to be carried away to the garage
so you can sit in your car?
Will you find comfort in rereading your
financial statement? Of course not.
What will matter then will be people.
If relationships will matter most then, shouldn't
they matter most now? —Max Lucado

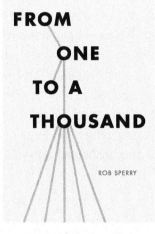

Download my free eBook on how to
never run out of contacts
www.robsperry.com/blueprint

CPSIA information can be obtained
at www.ICGtesting.com
Printed in the USA
LVOW13s1251050817
543916LV00019B/1425/P